The Contract On The Government

By Tommy Scott Hudson

©2013 Published by Tommy Scott Media, LLC
4141 Columbia Road, Suite C
Martinez, Georgia 30907

For Emerson

Table of Contents

Introduction – You Get What You Vote For!...............i

The Contract On The Government...........................1

Chapter 1. 3

Chapter 2. 23

Chapter 3. 34

Chapter 4. 53

Chapter 5. 65

Chapter 6. 73

Chapter 8. 95

Chapter 10. 131

Acknowledgments 139

About the Author 141

Introduction – You Get What You Vote For!

It is called the tipping point. Virtually everyone alive today learned of the tipping point as a part of childhood. That is, when the child is running across a field of grass with abandon and trips on his shoe lace. The child knows he is going to fall, but what does he do? He attempts to run harder to avoid the tipping point. The method of using speed to remain upright works for a few moments, but eventually gravity wins and the child either ends up with grass stains on his knees or a mouthful of sod.

This United States is doing much the same as the child attempting to avoid the inevitable fall. With some 16 trillion dollars of debt, a bloated and indecisive federal government and the apparent inability to slow the drain on the treasury, the government continues to print money in hopes that some economic miracle will occur and stave off the tipping point. However, my friends, gravity is not an abstract concept; gravity is a law and in the end gravity always wins.

Right now there are populist movements afoot nationwide. Some call themselves Tea Partiers and others call themselves Fair Taxers. Similar groups, like the Americans for a Balanced Budget Amendment, have gained momentum nationally. While the groups espouse some great ideas, no document or list of priorities binds them to cause a national spark and enact the changes they desire. There has been no politician that has come forward to offer any of these groups a road map to cause them to convene together and actually demand a set of priorities. People all over this country are discontent and they are beginning to see that the past policies of this nation are affecting their own wallets, yet they have no one standing before them offering any real solution that is not anything more than a meaningless catch phrase. And yes, I like Ron Paul and his Constitutionalist views, but sadly he is widely perceived as nuts.

Compounding the problem is a media that is so fractured intellectually and so consumed with ratings and sales that they have helped create an electorate that is now dominated by two different kinds of voters: the single issue voter and the uninformed voter. Neither can really be blamed for their actions at the polls. With the internet, the blogosphere, 500 television channels and radio dominated by political talk programming it is no wonder the electorate has been numbed into an army of robots.

The state of the country's finances is such a complex and confusing issue that it is virtually impossible to explain in a one minute news item, so the media turns its attention to other more emotionally charged stories that bring in ratings. Conservative media turns to scaring the wits out of gun owners while liberal media attempts to make every woman in the country think Republicans believe there is such a thing as legitimate rape.

What has happened is one segment of voters go to the polls with a single issue in mind and cast a vote based on that one issue. Even the most conservative minded gay people vote solely on who promises to allow them to marry. Meanwhile, pro-lifers vote for like minded candidates and those who are pro-choice vote for candidates who do not want to restrict abortions. Welfare recipients vote for who will continue to give them goodies, pot smokers vote for candidates who promise legalization of marijuana, Jewish people vote for anyone who supports Israel and the clinically insane vote for Roseanne Barr.

The other major segment of voters is those that have found themselves so awash in information and infotainment that they have simply begun to tune it all out. These are people who are tired of seeing the likes of pundits like Ann Coulter calling people fags on television, they know that Rachael Maddow despises rich people (even though she is rich herself) and that Rush Limbaugh is nothing more than a shill for the Republican party who basically produces a three hour infomercial for his tea company. It does get very tiring to try and discern if a news item on the internet is a factual piece of writing or a political advertisement. So the result is the over-informed changing the channel to Entertainment Tonight and become hopelessly uninformed.

Both of these segments of voters go to the polls knowing who they are going to vote for in one particular race and then speed through the rest of the list punching buttons so that they can get home in time to see if Brittney Spears has had another public meltdown. It is like they come to the table knowing they want to order a steak, but then mindlessly choose their appetizer, salad dressing, side dishes and desert. After dinner, they realize not only was the steak over cooked; but they found the ranch dressing was runny, the vegetables limp and the Baked Alaska was half-baked. Finally, they just decide not to eat out anymore and stay home.

A recent round of primary elections in my neck of the woods brought out yet another batch of news stories about low voter turnout. People cite all kinds of reasons for not going to the polls and generally those reasons have to do with what I just illustrated. Yet, by not participating in the process, otherwise successful and intelligent citizens are allowing other people to make decisions for them that directly affect their own bottom line. Either way, it is the combination of the single issue voter, the uniformed voter and the voter that stays home that has hurled this country towards the tipping point.

"I feel terrible about it," says South Carolina voter Gail Westerfield, who admits that while she did take the time to vote in the primary elections, she voted for a man because his name reminded her of her favorite soul singer. This otherwise informed person cast a vote for Democrat Al Greene, an unemployed man who lives with his father, didn't campaign for his Senate nomination, didn't raise any funding during the campaign and goes by the nickname of "Turtle." Anyone who has witnessed Greene speak aloud would agree the nickname is apt; Mr. Greene appears to be a little slow in the communication department.

"It's really scary to me," says Augusta, Georgia businessman and former elected official Joe Bowles speaking about how voters will either choose to stay home on important elections or cast a ballot out of pure ignorance. This man is an elected official and he is echoing what his colleagues are saying across the nation. Bowles not only manages his small business, but as a former local Commissioner he is keenly aware of just how much government at all levels impacts the ordinary individual's life. For a person in power in municipal government to be scared at the motivations and actions of the voters should be a wakeup call to every last legal American citizen living today.   What Bowles and other local-level elected officials see in their daily governmental business is indeed frightening. They know each dollar and cent spent by government at all levels is taken out of the wallets of taxpayers who are seeing their wallets wither and as a matter of consequence. It does not help when voters go to the polls and install ignorant people who do nothing other than continue a cycle that the study of world history proves to be disastrous.

On the national level, over 51% of voters punched a button to re-elect President Obama with many believing that he was going to force the rich to pay their fair share. Now, a good percentage voted for Obama for reasons other than taxes (because many of them do not pay taxes), but those who did vote on that single issue did so based on a promise encapsulated in a sound-bite. All it would have taken was for people to simply look past the slogan and listen to what the man actually said in speeches and in print to realize his "hope and change" was not taxing the rich alone. On January 1, 2013, Obama's working class voters found that "change" meant an extra $50 in federal payroll taxes per month for an employee making $30,000 a year.

On the local level in my city, the Obama wave swept in a city commission dominated by "progressives" who campaigned on helping the little guy. What was the first order of business for this progressive minded group? They pushed forward a "study" on how to tax the rain!

Taxes are embedded into everything, even the air we breathe and the amount of rain that falls. The price indicated on the electric and gas utility bill every business and every household receives is dictated by elected officials at the state and national level and yet very few people can name even one person who recently ran on a Republican or Democrat ticket for a Public Service Commission post. States are furloughing workers, cutting services, and finding unique new ways to raise taxes, yet hardly anyone outside of government can remember the name of their elected Secretary of State, Insurance Commissioner or Lieutenant Governor and those people did not win their offices without someone voting for them. How is it that a voter will elect someone they know nothing about and have no clue what decisions the person will make in office?

The people in public office make decisions that affect how business is conducted across the nation daily and yet most business owners refuse to take the time to involve themselves in local, state and even national politics. What is telling about the monumental struggles every state in the union is facing is the fact that many of the small amount of people who do take the time to go to the polls do not take a moment to inform themselves on the issues and the various candidate's positions on issues before they cast a ballot. One side of the electorate is apathetic and doesn't vote and the other side is completely ignorant and votes accordingly. Americans don't seem to care to become informed until their local school board cuts Pre-K programs because the state has run out of money and the daily household routine must suffer the consequence.

Years of voter apathy has resulted in people being elected to state and national office, voting on legislation and making national, state and local policy, who seem to be no more informed than the people who put them in office. The result is elected leaders like Nancy Pelosi saying Congress needs to vote on a bill so everyone can find out what the bill actually does. The American process of government from beginning to end, national down to local, has spun completely out of control. The final impact is now becoming what the actual taxpayers of this nation see as an iceberg looming in the distance. We are now all beginning to realize that the time of playing cards and enjoying highballs is over, the ship is about to be on the ice.

What is alarming today is the fact that many of the politicians themselves do not seem to know basic civics when it comes to the United States Constitution. That fact is precisely why our nation has moved so far away from the mandates of the US Constitution that we might as well not even have one at all. The people in power have almost no understanding of what the Federalist Papers suggest when examining the intent of the Constitution, rather, they attempt to interpret the document based on their own political needs. The result is a ruling class that is simply bent on ruling and not following the basic tenets that made this country a world power.

Recently, I was invited to participate in the Republican primary debates for the Georgia Public Service Commission on behalf of WGAC radio for Georgia Public Broadcasting. There were four men vying for the seat, three being former or current statewide elected officials and the final one being a long-time political activist. During the event, I asked several questions related to policy areas that each of the men were able to easily respond with the normal Republican rhetoric of cut taxes and cut spending. Then I threw the curve-ball question and none of them saw it coming. Since it was a Republican primary and not a general election with vastly different viewpoints being represented, I felt an ideological question was in order.

The question was prefaced with an explanation that the Georgia PSC must work with the federal government in almost all of its activities. The PSC, like almost every other agency of state government, is subject to unfunded mandates and regulations by the national government. Therefore, the question was, as conservatives, did the candidates favor a repeal of the 17th Amendment?

Candidate Joey Brush, a former Georgia state senator, was first to answer and it was clear from his body language that he really had no clue what exactly the 17th Amendment entailed. He smiled with a row of teeth that looked like piano keys as he struggled to respond.

"Is that a yes or no question?" He responded, obviously embarrassed.

The second response came from state Senator John Douglas who, almost angrily, argued that based on his being a student of history he felt the question had no merit. In a follow-up to his response, I asked if he felt, as a conservative, that state governments ought to have more of a voice in the federal government. Douglas remained defiant and refused to answer the question.

Then along comes a man named Tim Echols, a gentleman who had never been elected to public office but worked closely with the Christian Coalition and has been a political operative in Georgia for many years. In his answer, Echols veered off the charts and suggested America needed to adopt an amendment guaranteeing the right to life for the unborn before anyone looked at changing any other amendment. It stunned me that this candidate would bring abortion into a debate about the federal government's meddling into how much state regulated power companies charge for service. Since I was sitting in front of television cameras, I suppressed the impulse to vomit in public.

None of the three PSC candidates that had answered so far seemed to understand that the question was so simple, did they favor reducing the size of the federal government by giving the states back the voice they originally had under the Constitution, or not? It was a fair question to ask of people who call themselves conservative politicians.

The final candidate to respond, state Representative Jeff May, pulled out a copy of the Constitution and admitted that he had to look up the specific amendment. To his credit, at least May attempted to inform himself before blurting out an answer in front of televised state-wide audience.

The American system was built upon the concept called "layer-cake" federalism. Each level of government is meant to operate both independent of and rotating around all the various layers of local, state, and federal levels. The fact is that every one of the layers has some bearing on the average small citizen. It could be the bill received from the electric company or the local license inspectors' decisions or the fact that the federal government is attempting socialized government-run health care. Middle class Americans pay some form of a tax every time they turn on a light, pump gas, or purchase fishing supplies. Most people do not factor this in, but the amount of money spent nationally on the nation's defense impacts what happens down the governmental line and eventually ends at the door of the people who actually pay the taxes, meaning you and me.

"These are kitchen table issues," says Georgia State Representative May, who lost his bid for the PSC but remains devoted to energizing the average citizen to become more politically active. He says after 17 years in business, 6 years spent at the capitol in Atlanta, and a lifetime of being politically aware, he feels there is no more crucial time in American history since the Revolution that the people of this country need to be informed and vote with an informed mind. It goes beyond being liberal or being conservative, what it means is that people need to educate themselves on what the Constitution is and how it works.

May's statement that taxpayers simply suck it up and pay whatever bill they are hit with and little thought is given about how much money the government gets out of that bill is a bit simplistic. There is more to it than a simple misunderstanding of how government affects the pocketbook of the tax payer on a daily basis. It is not just the ignorance of voters or of the current political class, but common ignorance that America is operating on a system that has changed vastly from what was originally conceived by the men who fought and won the Revolution. If you, the reader, are a voter like Gail Westerfield or someone who cast a ballot for Barak Obama because of his lovely chocolate hue, then this book will likely be a waste of your time unless you are willing to change your behavior. If, though, you already have the basic understanding that every facet of your life is impacted by government and you are looking for solutions instead of some new slogan featuring a variation of the word "change," then you might get your money's worth with this little tome.

The Contract On The Government is a document inspired by one of the greatest minds ever to grace the countryside of North America. In writing this book, I used 'what would George Washington do' as the guiding principle. The following chapters lay out nine planks that I call Washingtonian Constitutionalism. Those nine planks are, in my somewhat learned opinion, the road map the populist groups are looking for.

The Contract On the Government can be the modern peoples definitive measure to do exactly what Mr. Washington did over 200 years ago, and that is wrestle tyranny into submission. Unfortunately for us, the stakes are much higher than they were in Washington's time, but by the good graces of God, we might prevail by applying the reason of people far smarter than us average folks. What is coming in the future is either Washingtonian Constitutionalism, or the dissolution of the republic known as the United States of America.

In our time, Washington and his contemporaries are not given the full credit due for their efforts in attempting to create a stable and responsive form of government that was intended to be accountable to the public at all levels. As we move along in trying to put the United States back on track, it is necessary to explore the areas that derailed the greatest republic ever formed for the benefit of humanity.

It is also important we know where we have been before we can chart where we should be going. We must also come to some hard conclusions about how we, as a people, allow our leaders to determine our individual destinies. We must face the fact that leaders in both major national parties are more concerned with maintaining their power and personal enrichment than committing themselves to the overall public welfare.

The Contract On The Government is my stand. It is a literary road map to making sure that future generations get a chance to participate in the republican arena created by George Washington and consecrated by the blood of our brave fore-bearers. To get there, we the people must have an understanding of why the Framers chose not a kingship, or a parliamentary government set-up or a democracy. We must understand why they labored over checks and balances to create the Constitution and America's unique form of federalism. Once we come to that understanding, then and then only can we discuss how to restore what they built and reclaim our public treasury.

The Contract On The Government

If We The People can accomplish these nine endeavors, together we will preserve the United States union for our children and we will prove to future generations that we acted as enlightened souls during our time spent on Earth.

1   **Repeal the 17th Amendment.**

2   **Give the President a Constitutional line item veto on budgetary matters.**

3   **Codify the War Powers Act as an Amendment and return national intelligence gathering responsibilities to the military in accordance to the Constitution.**

4   **Curtail domestic welfare by amending the Constitution granting voting rights to taxpayers only.**

5   **Curtail foreign welfare to be given only to emerging trading partners of the United States.**

6   **Withdraw totally from the United Nations and declare the U.S. a sovereign power with no permanent alliances.**

7   **Reduce the federal bureaucracy by eliminating all agencies that operate in violation of the 10th Amendment of the US Constitution and institute a 10% across the board fiscal budget cut of all federal agencies to reduce the size of the current federal government.**

8   **Establish an Amendment to the Constitution that declares the budget of the United States will, each year, will be balanced.**

9   **Establish a commission to examine and expose the details of legal segregation that occurred in the United States during the 19th and 20th centuries and give all parties immunity from prosecution.**

Chapter 1.
From Revolution to Progressive Reform to Hell

"I just don't know how they do it," my boss, Mary Liz, related to me about her daughter's softball game the afternoon before. The game had taken place in triple-digit temperatures. Mary Liz's daughter played catcher, so not only was she out in the broiling sun, but she was also covered head to toe in padding. The child must have been miserable. Her mother certainly was. Mary Liz told me she had to leave the game and go purchase a new T-shirt because the one she was wearing was drenched in sweat. It was not a fun wet tee-shirt contest for my News Director. On the field, her daughter Rachael must have been baking. Augusta, GA gets hot humid summers, so not only are you in an outdoor oven, but your body is basted as well.

Upon hearing the saga of the softball game-in-a-broiler, I reflected on what I had already planned as the beginning of this book. My thoughts went to the eras of American history I have been researching and I discovered a very common link. That is, we live in our reality and have little concept of the realities of the people who came before us.

After the ball game, those kids piled into a climate controlled vehicle, probably made a stop at Wendy's for a Frosty, and went home to a house with nice chilly air conditioning. Mary Liz was reflecting on how those kids could possibly handle such stifling heat, and my thought was, how could they handle it if they had none of the modern amenities we take for granted? Just 100 years ago people had literally none of the conveniences we enjoy today, yet they survived

3

just fine.

In 1910, there was no commercial air travel or satellites roaming the heavens. In those days, the thought of traveling to the Moon had not occurred to anyone, the Ottoman Empire was still around as were most of Great Britain's colonies and the greatest novelty and pleasure was the fact that one could sail the ocean in relative safety. It was a world many today have little understanding of as we enjoy the technological advantages of our time.

With the exception of scratchy newsreels shown on the Internet and period movies from Hollywood, the people of the 21st Century have little knowledge and understanding of the humans that lived the Edwardian era. Indeed, most people in 1910 still travelled on roads littered with horse dung and hung their laundry out to dry on a clothesline. Indoor plumbing was, like the telephone, an amenity for the wealthy. Most people performed their morning constitution in a smelly outhouse. They didn't flush, they had to spread lye.

We, as modern Americans, can no more fathom life in their time with no Wii, 900 channel television, radio or instant-connection-to-anyone-in-the-world-we-wish-to-connect-to anymore than Teddy Roosevelt would know what to do with an i-phone if we transported him to the future. We think we have it tough when we have to spend two hours outside of air conditioning and never think that 100 years ago there was no such a thing as indoor air.

It must be noted that the people of 1910 thought they were modern. They were building steel ships, drilling for oil, and dumping their industrial waste into every river they could find. This was also the time of the Progressive era in American politics, when society and government attempted to catch up with technology and Americans also began to turn to the federal government to fix the wrongs in the emerging industrial capitalist system. Times were difficult for them and decisions had to be made based on what they knew at the time. In hindsight, those folks during the Progressive administrations made a lot of errors. Those mistakes still resonate in the world of today and it is now time to acknowledge the mistakes and governmental overreaches and reverse them.

What we do not understand about the lives of turn of the century Progressives, they likely did not understand some of the same things about their fore-bearers. They felt they were modernizing the original Constitution based on the "living document" train of thought. To this day, America has continued to follow the policies of a by-gone time not realizing the progressive ideas about massive reform which included changing the original structure of the federal government was a hideous overreach that would eventually create the New Deal, the Great Society, and "wars" on everything imaginable. Those "reforms" have led us on a path that will eventually end in financial collapse, not a "fiscal cliff," mind you, but a collapse.

Just as Mary Liz and her kids (or me for that matter and you too most likely) could not imagine holding a softball game in the Georgia summer heat without the benefit of an air conditioner afterwards, the people of 1910 were disconnected from the lives of the people who lived a century before them. If turn of the 20th Century seem primitive to our modern eyes, the people of 1790 would have been considered just as primitive to those living in the Progressive era. Washington's age did not have telegraphs, freight trains, or electricity. The fact that electricity existed as a source of energy for people had only recently been discovered.

Progressives could not have conceived of why George Washington did not belong to a political party or why he thought political parties were a bad idea. Indeed, in his farewell address, Washington listed the political party as one of the "causes which may disturb our union." No one in the Progressive Era could have imagined life without political parties and that is because Washingtonian Constitutionalism had become passé by the turn of the 20th Century.

The people of 1910 were just discovering the ideas of Communism and Socialism and were reading stories about Anarchists over in Europe. Those Marxists ideals seemed like something that should be explored to a people who lived under dictates of the company store and were shocked at the writings of Upton Sinclair.

In those times, human achievement and technology began moving at a rate where it was outpacing society and many believed the government was there to help get everyone caught up. Mass advertising showed women how steam irons and vacuum cleaners could liberate them from the daily chores of the home and before long the women were using their newfound free time to demand to be allowed to vote. That is, those who could afford a steam iron.

America at the turn of the 20th Century did not have much of a middle class. Corporate barons lived in outrageously lavish mansions and securing a job as one of their servants meant you were middle class. The vast majority of people were poor, overworked, underpaid and either tied to the land or a grueling 80 hour week in a factory or mine. Progressive thinkers thought this was unfair and felt it was up to the government to right the wrong. However, rather than simply reform and regulate the workweek, end child labor and make other sensible regulations, they sought to make everyone equal in society. Equal, that is, for white folks. Only, what happened was that instead of making adjustments that strengthened the God given right to the pursuit of happiness, the "reformists" set the country on a track that eventually institutionalized poverty and drew the nation further into a society divided by class. And finally, those reforms have left this country financially bankrupt. We are becoming equal alright, equally miserable.

In Progressive era society, people began to really take note of how the overuse of alcohol destroyed families, created crime, and sickened people. They thought, perhaps for the first time in history, that the solution lied with the federal government and they banned all alcohol. History tells us that turned out to be a wild turkey of an idea.

It easy to see how during that time that the seed of this idea of a "living" Constitution began to grow into an organism that would change the structure of the federal government. When at first, the reforms of the Progressive era seemed to be producing positive results everyone but the robber barons cheered. But rather than sit back and smile at an accomplishment, the reformers ramped up and created more reforms. And that, my friends, is when everything slowly began to go down into the shitter.

Progressive people looked at the U.S. Senate as a group of elitists appointed by corrupt state governments, many of whom had only 50 years prior used their power to secede and spark the Civil War. The Progressives of the time began to see the framers of the Constitution as only semi-enlightened men – after all, they had slaves! They saw the Framers, whom they called the "Founding Fathers," as a group of paranoid paternalistic gentlemen who still practiced bloodletting and refused women the Franchise when they got together in Philadelphia and crafted the framework of "layer cake federalism," and its seminal documents the U.S. Constitution and The Federalist Papers.

Those inaccurate ideas about the men who created the United States persist to this day. In fact, most people only know George Washington for cutting down a cherry tree and being incapable of telling a lie. They know nothing of the struggle at Valley Forge or how many battles Washington and his men lost before finally tiring out the British Army and Navy. Indeed, it would come as a surprise to many that George Washington throughout his career never decisively won a military battle. Yet, he won the Revolutionary War. It is also never taught in schools that in Washington's time, women did have the right to vote as did anyone else who owned land. The same franchise was extended to free blacks that owned land as well. Did they tell you that in civics class?

Most people know that Thomas Jefferson had children with one of his slaves, Sally Hemmings. What they have not been taught is that Jefferson understood that slavery was an economic model that would eventually fold in on itself. It wasn't sustainable. Most people today do not know that the original Library of Congress began with books sold to the government by Jefferson to pay his enormous debts because his plantation could not fully support itself based on mass slave labor. In his autobiography, Jefferson wrote, "I made one effort in that body [House of Burgesses] for the permission of the emancipation of slaves, which was rejected." Yes, Jefferson tried throughout his entire life to end the cycle of slavery, but revisionist historians seem to only want to focus on his attraction to one of his bondwomen.

Revisionists want to paint the heroes that created this nation with a broad brush and ignore the fact that nearly every man who signed the Declaration of Independence either died in the Revolution or died shortly afterwards riddled with debt and living in poverty. Those men sacrificed their lives so that future generations could eventually sit at a computer and order the latest technological device on-line without interference from a government.

It is flat out amazing to me that people who call themselves historians and political scientists will twist the truth of what happened two hundred years ago and sell it to a public that has now become accustomed to a government that operates in direct contradiction of the Constitution it is sworn to uphold. The media of our age is also not interested in painting an accurate picture, but rather they deliver a distorted image that is really nothing more than a collection of lies. The sad fact is that many of them know exactly what they are doing and they do it anyway.

Modern political blogger Sally Kohn recently wrote the following for the Huffington Post: "The vaunted leaders at the Constitutional convention were all very wealthy, very white men and included the largest slave owners in the colonies. None of the Founders were very pro-equality on the subject of race, but some were more opposed to slavery than others. In particular, the North was more opposed to slavery than was the South. And the North had more people. So the

South was worried that, if the new nation were just based on the popular vote alone, it would have less power and slavery would be abolished. They created a Constitution to preserve slavery, with all sorts of compromises to appease the South and keep it – and slavery – in the union."

Yeah, and all the people of 1910 drove Cadillacs and had air conditioning and a computer in every home.

The truth is many of those men, John Adams for one, never in their lives owned slaves. The ones that did own slaves, like Thomas Jefferson, inherited most of their slaves and were caught in a hideous financial bind they detested. How do you release something the bank considers to be property? It is hurtful and an awful conclusion to have to draw, but it is the truth that slaves were considered property in the time of Washington and Jefferson. To just go out and whole stock set everyone free would have been tantamount to releasing a herd of prized livestock according to the ones who controlled the economy of the times. Washington and Jefferson were born into that system; they did not create it.

While I can certainly agree with Kohn that the framers lived in a completely different world than we do today where slavery was tolerated, her words echo what I hear coming from others like her who simply refuse to research for themselves and rather accept revisionist history as the truth. The same mentality occurred during the Progressive era and their "reforms" led us down a path that has dead-ended into an imperial presidency, a bankrupt central government, and a Constitution that is now being published with a disclaimer as if it might contain porn within its pages.

The United States government of today looks nothing like the government born of quill and parchment by the original founders. The transformation has been slow and deliberate, instigated at first by what was considered common need and continued on today by people who are on record as saying they abhor the men who gave their lives to create this union.

Modern political pundit Glenn Beck has made a career out of voicing his disgust with progressive President Woodrow Wilson. Much of Beck's bile targeted at Wilson is deserved and modern progressives go out of their way to deny the facts surrounding this man. Again, rather than read the truth that was published during Wilson's time and doing a little rudimentary research on his boyhood, modern progressive thinkers venerate Wilson and his eventual successor FDR as modern day "Founding Fathers." People ignorant to history treat Jefferson and Washington as slave drivers, but refuse to recognize the fact that Jim Crow legal segregation in the South went from de facto to de jour under Wilson and yet he remains the hero of modern Progressives.

Thomas Jefferson wanted to include language in the Declaration of Independence blaming the King for slavery in America and that fact is not taught in public schools. Neither is the fact that the most impassioned defense of slavery was delivered from the pulpit of First Presbyterian Church of Augusta, Georgia by one Joseph Ruggles Wilson, father of the future President Wilson during the so-called Progressive era. Joseph Wilson argued shortly before the Civil War that slavery was the commandment of God, and his son Thomas Woodrow Woodrow was in the audience when those words were spoken.

Thomas Jefferson wrote of the moral repugnance of slavery, and dreamed of the day when economics would allow him to free the slaves he had inherited as property. Meanwhile, the Great Reformer Wilson would go on to preside over the most shameful era of American race relations: segregation and third class citizenship for people of color.

What is generally not discussed is that the men who framed the Constitution fought more than just the Revolution and the War of 1812. Great Britain was not the only world power interested in North America during those turbulent times. These same men who would later spend 40 days in the sweltering heat of a locked down building in Philadelphia that did not have television and movies for entertainment between work sessions. So instead, they read these interesting little paper rectangles called books. They knew from reading of the Greeks and Romans and Ottomans and Egyptians that pretty much every form of government tried up to that time eventually ended in failure. Kings became despots, dynasties became corrupt (and sometimes in-bred) and tiny city-states became enormous unmanageable empires. As the Framers of the Constitution worked on crafting a future political system, they studied every type of system that had been tried in the past.

It wasn't just the tyrannical actions of the King of England they feared being committed by a future American government, but they were aware how the cycle of how any amount of political power eventually creates tyranny unless checks and balances constantly hem it in. They also studied the current world political climate of the time by receiving bits and pieces of news from overseas. During the time the Constitution was being drafted, the Framers could see what a political powder keg existed in ally France and feared the same thing could happen in the new United States. Even though some of the most brilliant political thinkers of the time hailed from France, by 1789 it was clear that what had once been the most stable monarchy in Europe was crumbling fast and the country was headed into civil war.

The framers understood the reasons for what was happening in France; a strong central government led by incompetent heads of state had mired itself in wars and debt. Even as bread became scarce to the citizenry, the government still partied like it was 1799. And sure enough, history tells us what followed was bloodshed. Ironically, it was the French monarchy that had earlier bankrolled the American Revolution.

The framers of the U.S. Constitution sought to form not a perfect union, but a more perfect union because they understood that absolute perfection does not exist within humanity. Each level, each separate component of the union's evolving structure was debated both orally and through letters. They discussed every imaginable contingency; how and under what circumstances any of the separate branches could spiral into tyranny. In the end, they crafted a short, to the point document they felt if followed to the letter would provide not a democracy, but a government by the people. It was something that had never been thought of before, a representative constitutional republic with checks and balances at every level. The U.S. Constitution created something that had not ever been dreamed by any of the smartest men in all of humanity. It created the concept of dual sovereignty, or as stated before, the idea layer-cake federalism.

The goal was that politics and issues dealing most with the average citizens everyday lives would be decided at the local level. The county or city council of a town or city would really interact more with the mass citizenry than the representatives of the national government. At the next level up, officials of the several sovereign states would also have more interaction with the common citizen than the officials of the national government. In fact, the original Constitution only allows for members of the House of Representatives to be directly elected by the people. It was the idea of the working tiers that would allow each to perform its assigned function and create efficiency and accountability while making it impossible for any faction to become totally supreme.

Cities handle local zoning variances and collect the trash, states craft criminal law and build roads, and the national government delivers the mail, prints money, negotiates treaties, and defends the nation against armed attack. The original ideas and Constitution that cemented them is so complex, yet so brilliantly simple. At less than 5000 words, the Constitution succinctly lays out a blueprint for a national government presiding over sovereign states and sovereign people and it guards against both an aggressive militarized national state and one that could become so weak and ineffectual that it would eventually collapse from its own weaknesses.

The Constitution also did another important thing. In the minds of the ruling classes from Caesar's time to that of King George was the concept of ever expanding power for the state. Leaders had to conquer land and people to consolidate power and then would go on another conquest to cement the cycle. The people governed never had a say in the matter and as long as things were going well they generally didn't care. The masses felt they were protected by a powerful ruler and as long as their daily lives were not disrupted, then they let the king rule how he wanted. After all, the concept was people did not give consent to be governed; power flowed from the state, not to it from the very ones supporting it with their money.

Rather than seek to consolidate and expand, the Constitution did just the opposite. It created semi-autonomous regions called states and made the national government the mechanism that bound the states together. Instead of a king, with the God given right to rule, the Constitution would for the first time in humanity codify the notion that people give their consent to be governed. The benchmark thought was that government does not own itself and the elite do not own the government, but all of the people who pay taxes have the right to consent to be governed. The result of those basic ideological cornerstones did not create a democracy, but a government structure based on democratic ideals.

Then some very well meaning people had to go screw it all up. The Progressive thinkers of the early 20th Century only considered what was going on in their time, not what preceded them or what might occur in the future. They never stopped to think about why the Framers wrote the Constitution the way they did and how the mechanisms of government really worked. The Progressive movement did not take into account all the deliberation that went into the document called the Constitution or what was going on during the lives and times of the people 100 years before. They also did not take into account what their reform actions might create 100 years into the future.

Today, we are seeing the effects of the Progressive thinker's knee jerk reactions and those reactions in the form of amendments, laws and ever expanding federal government agencies will continue to impact the next century of American life unless the current populace moves to revisit those decisions and abolish some of them.

I tend to try to avoid using the modern pundit-loaded words conservative and liberal. Those words, in my view, have lost their meaning and have become nothing other than slurs the politicos like to hurl at one another. This book has not been written by a person that considers himself a Republican or a Democrat, because as I will illustrate herein, there is no longer any difference between the two parties. I personally believe in the Constitution and a policy of reason that was founded by George Washington who belonged to no political party. In this day and time, our two national political parties have more in common in their motives than they have ideologies separating them. What they have in common is the pursuit and growth of political power and what separates them is nothing other than vague words and silly slogans. Instead of calling the parties Republican and Democrat, you might simply call them Boss and Hogg.

In my estimation, if you want to use the code words, the last liberal president we had was George W. Bush (Barak Obama doesn't count, he is a confirmed socialist) and the last conservative President to sit in the oval office was John Kennedy. Sorry friends, Ronald Reagan spent more than he saved. It is true that Reagan was at heart a conservative, but his inability to see the Soviet Union would eventually collapse on its own led to a massive build up of this nation's military industrial complex. That fact all by itself is a bad thing.

It is also important to add that I have been to several Tea Party events, but I was there as a journalist and not as a participant. I am not a Tea Party member, but I have observed the movement. In my observation of these rally events and others like them combined with the subsequent media coverage, I see that people know something is bad wrong with the national government in this country. A communist nation owns our national debt and if Mexico doesn't eventually annex the state of California, the state is going to collapse into bankruptcy.

America is bleeding money in the form of welfare to both foreign nations, U.S. citizens and illegal aliens and we are bleeding real blood overseas in shooting wars that have real no end in sight. Dynasties have been created with two families either controlling or occupying high positions in the executive branch for decades, Federal Senators are being re-elected for life, Supreme Court justices are chosen based on their loyalty to anything other than the Constitution, congressional representatives no longer attempt to hide the fact that lobbyists and unions buy their votes and the end result is the only people really motivated to vote are the ones who know they will get something out of the deal.

Federal lawmakers of today pass laws they admit they did not draft and did not read. "Public servants" have been caught on tape roughing up college students for merely asking their stand on an issue and the federal government refuses to allow states to patrol their own borders and turn out illegal aliens all to the yawn of a people who long ago decided their vote doesn't really count. What the disgruntled haven't learned is that the ones actually voting on a regular basis are the very people a sane citizenry should be worried about. The segment of society that votes most here is the segment that does not pay taxes and are dependent on the government. The non-taxpayers are in control because they are willing to vote and they know their vote counts more because other people do not take out the time to vote even when it is their hard earned money that is on the table for the taking. So, you can say we have a true democracy now, only is it power in numbers or mob rule?

What is happening now is exactly what the Framers feared and tried to prevent: tyranny by the masses. Right now, the masses of people that do not pay money into the system of government are the very ones making the decisions at the ballot box.

Sadly, there is more to add to the list of the American people's troubles. Massive federal bureaucracies like the Department of Housing and Urban Development (HUD) suck up tax money and spit it out to state agencies that, in turn, give it to quasi-governmental agencies (Community Housing Development Organizations or CHoDOs). Not surprisingly, when the money never makes it to the intended recipients there is no accounting for where the money went. Buckling under federal unfunded mandates, states cannot make their payrolls without furloughing employees, fix aging infrastructure or even cut the grass alongside the highways. Money needed by the states for daily operation is being hurled by the federal government in the exact opposite direction.

Thanks to a ridiculous policy known as the War on Drugs, urban areas are ruled by gangsters worse than Al Capone (Capone only killed other gangsters while the drug lords of Chicago today kill children), prisons are overcrowded with pot dealers, and there are more drugs on the streets today than ever before. All of the above has gone unnoticed by the general population until now, but the political leaders refuse to blame national drug policy and instead blame the proliferation of guns. Make no mistake, no matter your feelings on the 2nd Amendment, it is the billions of dollars the government spends "fighting" drugs that has ruined more lives and killed more people than any shiny piece of metal that fires bullets. The fact is the war on drugs has not only made the drug problem worse, it has drained the treasury.

Speaking of war, the latest decades long "War on Terror" has eclipsed Vietnam as being America's biggest military blunder. Afghanistan and Iraq continue to be unstable hotbeds of terrorist activity, the State Department continues to call the country that harbored and protected Bin Laden a "friend," and what was initially sold to the American public as a spread of democracy has turned out to be the legitimization of Al Qaeda through the "Arab Spring." In the face of mistake after mistake which has led to thousands of lives lost including that of an American ambassador, the government continues blunder on as if it were winning the fight.

Once the dust settled in Egypt, true political scientists stopped celebrating the ouster of President Hosni Mubarak and began admitting that America had lost a key ally in the Middle East. Almost immediately the new Egyptian government denounced Israel, voted in a constitution based on Islamic law and began arresting Christians. In response, what did the American government do? It sent sixteen F-16 fighter aircraft and two hundred Abrams tanks! The past nonsensical policy of arming "friendly freedom fighters" that ultimately turned out to become the enemy was abandoned for the absolutely insane policy of directly arming the enemy.

Trust me, people are now noticing this nation has gone off the rails, but they just do not know what to do to fix the situation. Where in the past, voting was the answer; it has now become part of the problem. When people are forced to vote for the lesser of two evils, they are still voting for evil and people are beginning to wake up and come to terms with that fact.

This country's spiral away from its founding principles is now hitting Americans hard in the collective bank account; only this time we do not have a Hitler to cause a war that will solve the economic crisis. War overseas, War on Poverty, War on Drugs, over-regulation in some areas and under-regulation in others, massive borrowing, a wasteful and unfair tax code and able body citizens being allowed laze around on the public dole have pushed America to the brink of certain disaster.

The national media lives in the day and not what might be in the future, and the result is a further numbing-down of an otherwise intelligent electorate. News programmers do not want to spend five minutes explaining what "monetizing the debt" means when they can focus more attention on the outrageous performer Lady Gaga's latest outfit and score ratings from the ignorant morons that pay more attention to commercials than the content of real news. Everyone knows that actress Lindsay Lohan was in rehab, but few realize that if the federal government does not go into financial rehab then hardly anyone soon will be able to afford a ticket to a Lohan movie when she makes her big comeback.

It must be noted that financial over-extension (not Reagan) is what brought down the USSR just as it was before what brought down the Tsar in Imperial Russia. Financial over-extension brought down the French crown and plunged that country into prolonged bloodshed. Well over two thousand years ago, Cicero tried to warn Rome during his day, writing:

"The budget should be balanced; the Treasury should be refilled, public debt should be reduced, the arrogance of officialdom should be tempered and controlled, and the assistance to foreign lands should be curtailed lest Rome become bankrupt. People must again learn to work, instead of living on public assistance."

No one listened to Cicero and as we know from history, financial over-extension and the inability to secure their borders brought down the glory of the Roman Empire. In fact, history is littered with examples of once august civilizations brought down not by outside conquest, but by financial overextension.

As a journalist, I see that people on the street are getting angry. Callers to talk radio are getting more and more desperate because they can hear rhetoric but find no real leaders to back the rhetoric. The most extreme among us are hoarding guns and food waiting for a collapse that can be prevented. From the rallies I have been to, it has become clear to me that the people of the United States are beginning to wake up and realize that not only did they get drunk and puke on the minister at the reception, but that they married a whore.

Washington, Franklin, Madison and Jefferson et al. gave us a framework and the framework is still there, it is just that our leaders refuse to follow it. Therefore, as others have recently said publicly, we as a people must now choose to take the power back by whatever means is necessary. In that, we as a people have two choices and that is to take that power back violently or find a way to do it peacefully. I vote we do it peacefully. However, the ballot box is proving to be an empty solution at the federal level. As long as the ones in power have their perks, they care little about what we think. Furthermore, as long as those in power are propped up in part by a minority of citizens that depend on them for daily subsistence, more and more responsible tax payers are going to give up and stay home on election day.

While it may seem I am railing against liberals, think again about the Republican side as they have proven to adopt the same level of arrogance when their party gets to step up (or waddle) to the plate. Republicans and Democrats have different logos and catch phrases, but they employ the same modus operandi when in office.

Moving forward, the process cannot follow through the traditional means of the political party. Over the years I have seen too many good men and women get sucked into the party machinery and either end up morally disgraced or jailed for committing a crime while in office. All politicians pander to constituencies but most fail to bring about any result other than either their own personal enrichment and/or the enrichment of their party. It is time for Americans to demand some changes and it is time for our leaders to both adhere to the Constitution and fix the flaws the Progressive Era created or tell us to our face they have no intention of ever doing so and allow us to switch to plan B and start talking secession. Either way, our time demands a revolution.

Things will not change at the federal level until the people organize at the state level and then collectively demand change of the national government by way of enforcing the law. The United States Constitution is our first, last, and only hope for survival as a nation. We, as a people must restore the original document and remove some of the "progressive" amendments and laws that have been codified in the past. Now is the time for America to pick ourselves back up and learn from the past mistakes as we chart a course for the future. The tipping point is no longer on the horizon, it is here now.

It is time for America to deal with problems in America and let the rest of the world deal with their own issues without the United States having to be the world's fundraiser and policeman as well. It is time for the common American to learn the history of this nation and it's framework of government on their own without relying on pundits like Rachael Maddow, Bill O'Reilly, Keith Olbermann, or Rush Limbaugh to be their primary source of information. At this critical juncture, you, the common American, must turn off "Dancing With The Stars" and pick up a copy of The Federalist Papers.

America does not need a new Constitution, nor does it need suffer another violent revolution. The United States will not have another Civil War for one simple reason: if directed to do so, the military's generals will not order their troops fire on fellow Americans. American Generals as well as privates in the Army tell me if Texas decides to become its own republic, they will not obey orders to kill in order to stop it from happening.

Before you begin to believe I am one of those running around with a tinfoil hat, hording supplies, stockpiling ammunition and digging my own well in the back yard; I want you to consider what happened in the country of Romania in the waning days of the Soviet Union. In the 1960's, a man by the name of Nicolae Ceausescu came to power in that communist nation. His first act was to defy the USSR over their military aggressiveness and declare his state independent of Moscow. Nicolae Ceausescu became the darling of Western leaders who proclaimed him "the good communist."

Now, I am not mixing apples with oranges by comparing the current plight of the United States with the history of a communist state. Romania at that time was a repressive communist state with a leader that adored North Korea's Kim Jung Il. The comparison comes when you investigate what Ceausescu did with his nations' economy and how the house of cards eventually caved in.

Romania in the 1960's was a poor nation that relied primarily on agriculture. By warming up to Western leaders, Ceausescu was able to secure massive loans to industrialize his country. The "stimulus package" he received led to the building of factories and roads. People were moved from the fields into the cities. Unemployment in Romania became almost unheard of and everyone had a car, an apartment, access to free healthcare and a guaranteed state provided vacation. The people loved Ceausescu and for two decades worshiped him like a god.

However, Ceausescu had used the "stimulus" money to invest in infrastructure that became obsolete almost from the moment it was built. Rather than realize his mistake, Ceausescu borrowed more and more money and used vast sums of it to raze the historic district of Bucharest and build the largest government complex and palace in the world. When the loan notes came due, Ceausescu realized his credit limit had been reached and was forced to begin emptying the already empty treasury to settle the debts.

Rolling electrical blackouts began to occur across the country, but through the state run media, Ceausescu was able to rally his countrymen claiming the austerity measures were temporary. Television programs showed him touring factories and posing in front of markets filled with food. What no one knew was that it was all a façade. The factories were not operational and the items on the fruit and vegetable stands were made of wax.

Prior to the Romanian economic collapse, British officials saw a chink in the armor but kept quiet. Ceausescu had agreed to purchase a fleet of British aircraft. When he visited the UK to seal the deal, he tried to negotiate to pay for the planes with several ship loads of oranges. Needless to say, the British declined the offer.

Ceausescu managed to keep up the façade until the bitter end. As the Warsaw Pact began to unravel, the political commentators of the time almost unanimously agreed as communist governments fell that Ceausescu was immune to the growing discontent and would be the one communist dictator to remain in power. After all, what the West saw on television were parades in Ceausescu's honor and adoring crowds holding his picture and chanting his name.

Romania continued to send its food away to pay its debts, the blackouts continued and finally the public began to realize they had been duped. People across the country were starving while Ceausescu and his wife had food tasters and footmen at their service. Riots erupted throughout the country and in the space of a few days Ceausescu was deposed, tried and executed.

Understand that I am not saying a President of the United States could face such a similar fate. What I am saying is that our country is playing the same economic shell game. By borrowing to stimulate a stagnant economy, this country is doing the same thing the leaders of Romania did. As long as the leaders of Romania avoided the tipping point, the public followed without question. However, no matter how firm a grip the government had on power, it could not survive when hungry and angry citizens took to the streets. When the government ordered the military to forcefully stop the protests, the military said "no" and turned on the government. Romanian solders refused to fire on their own countrymen.

Similarly, there will never be another Kent State massacre in America. If a state like Texas feels they have had enough and declares themselves a republic, the American military will not lift a finger or a gun to stop them.

The alternative is the Contract On The Government. To implement the Contract, the people must do more than simply vote at election time. The organized protests such as the Tea Parties and Fair Taxers must become even more organized and take the Contract On The Government to the state capitals. From there, the people must demand their U.S. Senators convene a Constitutional Convention enacting the proposals as set forth and all of it can be done with a couple of amendments that rescind the poor choices of the past. The original U.S. Constitution must be restored as the blueprint for American governance. Once the needed amendments are ratified by the states, the people and the states should demand the other non-amendment provisions of the Contract be enacted through legislation.

Will this process take years? Yes. Is it radical? Yes. Is it necessary? Yes, unless you want your grandchildren living in a loose confederation of sovereign countries that once comprised the United States of America because I can guarantee you that is exactly where this country is headed. When less than 50% of the citizens in this nation pay income taxes and those that don't pay taxes receive money from the government as an incentive to vote for those who will give them more, we are, as a nation, headed for disaster. When a nation becomes an empire that is fighting undeclared wars on no less than 3 fronts in the face of many other nations doing everything they can to increase global instability, that nation is headed toward disaster. When a nation allows a tiny cabal of people to usurp the reins of government and rule with elite indifference to the citizenry, that nation is headed toward disaster. Finally, just ask the English crown, when a population feels it lives as a people taxed without representation, the government is headed for disaster.

No, the time for talking is over. It is now time for action. It is time to tell the politicians the citizenry has had enough of the empty catch phrases and slogans and we demand they do what they promised to do before they became elected. It is time to truly take our country out of the hands of the tyrants and give it back to whom it belongs· the people. It is time to put out a Contract On The Government.

In my media career, the major test for any news story is based on the question of what would the reasonable person infer? To use the cliché, I am asking would the reasonable person infer the animal placed before them is goose or a duck? Depending on size, color, and shape, most people can tell the difference between the two birds.

With the Constitution, it is really very easy to apply that test. The document is short and to the point. The phrase "general welfare" means the welfare of everyone, not a select group. General welfare means you have the right to purchase a house that is hooked up to a public sewage system that prevents to spread of disease, but it does not give you or your neighbor the RIGHT to be given free housing. Meanwhile, the 10th Amendment was written in English, not Yiddish, so when it says that "powers not delegated to the United States by the Constitution, nor prohibited by it to the states, are reserved to the states respectively, or to the people", then it means just that. No one should have to translate the sentence to explain its meaning: if the Constitution does not specifically give the federal government a power, then it does not have that particular power.

The important thing is that the framers added in the amendment process knowing things would indeed change after they were gone and the people needed a mechanism to adapt to the changes. What this book is attempting to do is simply apply a little reason to the problems facing this country and offer the solutions. Some solutions are in the form of an amendment, and the others are just applying a little common sense.

Common Sense, that was a book once, wasn't it? Oh, it was just a pamphlet, sorry.

Chapter 2.
I Hate Democracy! (And You Should Too!)

That got your attention, didn't it? There is a big difference between holding democratic principles as sacred and believing democracy is a sensible form of government. Believe it or not, I actually had college professors refer to the United States as "the world's greatest democracy." We are not now and have never been a democracy. The United States is a constitutional representative republic not a democracy, and there is a huge difference between the two.

If pure democracy were put in practice it would be far worse than communism. In fact, I shock my friends by telling them I believe communism is the greatest form of political structure ever conceived on paper. They relax when I go on to say communism is a utopian fantasy that can never actually be fulfilled. With communism, every time it has been tried, and pure Marxist communism has never been tried because that is impossible (it looks good on paper but in reality is impossible to institute), it has lead to totalitarianism. What makes democracy worse is that not only does it lead to totalitarianism, but it can also lead to anarchy. It is funny that I recently heard this same argument being made on the air by a radio talk show host. I am now wondering how my college papers got leaked to the now retired Neal Boortz. With that assertion, I jest, but Boortz equated democracy with mob rule and he could not be more correct on the matter.

The framers of the U.S. Constitution feared democracy; they honestly felt it would likely be better to stick with England before embarking on something that would eventually become mayhem. Rather, they produced a document that very delicately balanced three interests: the administration of a sovereign central government, the administration of sovereign state governments, and the needs and interests of a sovereign people.

The points that made it all work operated on a pivot, and the central points are as such: the President is to be elected by special electors drawn from the population of states (NOT the people at large), the Senate members are to be elected by the legislatures of the states (NOT the people at large), and the Supreme Court, the only specific court mentioned in the Constitution, is to be appointed by the President and approved by the Senate (NOT the people at large). So where are We The People in all of this? Easy, the federal body chosen directly by the People is the House of Representatives. See how that works?

Since the People elect the leaders of states, municipalities, boards, commissions, and authorities, we are already broadly represented. In fact, no other country in the world has as many elected positions throughout its form of government.

The individual 50 states were set up to be and remain today semi-sovereign entities like mini-countries. States have militias, they pass laws, they collect taxes, they build infrastructure, they have a police and judicial system and they have borders. Under the "shared-sovereignty" approach in the Constitution, states gave up the right to raise armies (which are different from militias), print money, operate on deficits, and enter into treaties with foreign powers.

So, where did the wheels fall off the Duisenberg? When did the design of the original structure become almost irreparably altered? Well it was when some genius thought it would be wise to make America more of a democracy and call for the direct election of U.S. Senators.

Thanks to the 17th Amendment, federal Senators are no longer representatives of the state government from which they originate, but representatives of the People, or the politicozombies, as I like to call them. The people elected to represent at the state level and are responsible for the day to day running of the state have nothing to say about the actions of the federal government because no one in Congress represents them. The very people who must daily deal with the draconian excesses and dictates of the federal government have the same number of votes as the rest of the sheeple: one.

Think of it this way, the Constitution set up a table balanced on three legs and the 17th Amendment removed one of those legs. Now for such a table not to tumble over, it is necessary for someone to physically hold it up with their hands. We have been propping up the table with our tax money and the problem is that more and more items keep being placed on the table. Tax money, like physical strength, is finite. At some point, the table will come crashing down. What all this means in the real world, is that it does not matter if the person in office as President has the last name of Obama, Roosevelt, or Hudson. It also doesn't matter if Democrats or Republicans control the federal government, the end result is the same. Having no vote in federal matters means the several states must abide by whatever dictate comes down from on high.

In the latest election, the good folks of Puerto Rico voted in a nonbinding referendum to apply for statehood. I can't help but to think those people are every bit as crazy as the gay folks who want to get married. Demanding to be allowed to be miserable like everyone else is lunacy to me. Right now, the Puerto Ricans do not have representation in Congress, but neither does the 50 states.

The individual states no longer have a voice or a vote in the process and that means every decision of the feds must be followed by the state governments and paid for by the citizens of that state. Now I know that the term 'states rights' brings up images of the Civil War, but as semi-sovereign entities, states do deserve the right of representation. The federal Senate was supposed to be an institution that represents the concerns of the individual states, but it not any longer.

Right now, it is states that are subject to taxation without representation in the form of regulatory directives and unfunded mandates. Thanks to the 17th Amendment, the federal government can come in with things like No Child Left Behind, which has all of these wonderful mandates on instituting certain curriculum and after school projects but gives the state no budget for putting the programs in place. The money has to come from somewhere and states can't run deficits. Now do you see why state education across the country is in such a mess?

The feds will give a state an unreasonable amount of time to bring air quality standards to a certain level. The state does not have the time, or the funding, to study and develop alternative energy plans and does not have the authority to do certain things like build a nuclear plant. So, instead they are forced to create a band-aid in the form of "boutique blends" of gasoline to meet the standards and avoid a fine (tax). States also are severely restricted from oil exploration on their own territory and they do not have the power to regulate companies like British Petroleum drilling off their shores. Now do you see why gasoline is so expensive? And who would you prefer to be the ones to inspect those off shore rigs, the feds with their abysmal track record, or the states like Louisiana and Mississippi whose land and seas are the ones threatened with spilled oil in case of a disaster like the one that just recently occurred in 2010? Hindsight sure is 20/20 isn't it?

Naturally, unfettered freedom would be as bad as the harsh regulation with no state input we have right now, but if the states had a representative arm in the national government like they originally did, then the size and scope of the national government would shrink considerably and become more proactive. States would also have a much better ability to work together to solve regional issues rather than wait for Big Brother to tell them what to do.

The modern Senate is nothing but a smaller version of the House of Representatives; only the members get six year terms and tend to stay in office well past the time normal people would be retired in an assisted living facility. In fact for some, like the late South Carolina Senator Strom Thurmond, the Senate was an assisted living facility with him voting from his hospice bed. In fact, Thurmond is a great case study on how it is not wise to give the people too much voting power. Thurmond won term after term in his heyday even though he was an ardent segregationist. He won more Senatorial terms as a "reformed" segregationist who slept with the help and married a woman young enough to be his grandchild. Thurmond continued to win terms even when it was clear to South Carolinians that the man was senile. After 48 years of public "service", it was the grim reaper rather than voters that finally removed that man from office.

I once asked Georgia Senator Johnny Isakson why, as a conservative, he did not champion the repeal of the 17th Amendment. His response to me was that the Senate is "a more deliberative body." Okay, so what then is the House of Representatives, pray-tell? Are they a bunch of kindergartners running around drawing up legislation with crayons? Wait, don't answer that.

Modern Senators form political coalitions based on party, not on needs of their state. Sure, House members also form party coalitions, but that is a healthy thing, they were voted in office in most cases based on their identification with their political party. If they side with their party against their constituents, then they get voted out in two years. So why shouldn't Senators do the same? Because the whole idea of creating a Senate was that it would represent THE STATES, not the people, and not the party of their affiliation.

You might point out a Republican state assembly would appoint a Republican Senator and Democrat assemblies would send Senators of their party, so there is no way to take out party politics. The difference is the people of the state voted in the party of the state so the legislature would then send the representative of their choice to represent them. If a change occurs in the state and the opposite party takes over, then the new party gets to choose the Senators. So simple, Senators should be there to look after the needs of the state, not the people who fund their political party and certainly not themselves and their campaign war chests.   The framers thought of the Senate as grouping of diplomats representing the interests of the region in which they live as a whole. If a Representative draws up a piece of reasonable legislation, then attaches riders that sneak unreasonable sums of money to his constituents for vanity projects, then it should be Senators who strike that language from the bill before it ever reaches the President. In fact, it should be Senators that champion the effort to constitutionally control the use of riders and earmarks altogether.

If a bill such as No Child Left Behind passes the House, then it should be Senators that ask themselves 'where is the funding for this?' If the bill contains unfunded mandates that would be an unfair burden on the states, then they must protect their state by voting against it. Likewise, when the federal government violates the 10th Amendment with a national health care plan, the Framers designed a mechanism to prevent states having to sue the federal government over the issue and that mechanism is the Senate.

Illegal immigration would still be a problem, but it would be a problem for the individual states as well as the federal government. Under the Constitution, a person is a citizen of the state in which they reside and a citizen of the United States. Therefore, an illegal alien is not only violating federal law when he/she/he-she/she-he (see, I'm politically correct) enters the country illegally, h/s/h-s/s-h is also violating a state law. When faced with what can only be described as an invasion across the borders, the Senators of Georgia, Texas, and Arizona should be in Washington D.C. demanding the federal government aid them in repelling the invasion. After all, the people crossing the border are not just pretending to be US citizens; they are pretending to be state citizens. Not only are they not paying federal taxes, but also they are not paying state taxes! Not only are they getting federal handouts, but they are also getting state benefits.

Even though it seems to make perfect sense, US Senators are not going to support a repeal of the 17th Amendment. When the amendment was sold to the people, it was presented as a means of giving the people more power over the national government. Naturally, the people bought into the concept of being able to vote for their Senator. What some didn't realize and others craftily forgot to mention, was that the 17th Amendment actually did was make Senators no longer responsible to the state they served. Instead, they are beholden only to themselves, the bloc that voted for them and the special interest groups that gave them money. Once a person is elected to the Senate they have a near 90% chance of being reelected for as long as they wish to serve. Have you ever wondered how a person can leave their job, have roughly $200,000 in their personal savings account, travel to Washington and six years later be a millionaire?

Money is the reason hardly none of the Senators want to see a repeal of the 17th Amendment. Liberal commentators love to point out how Republicans are cozy with Big Oil and Big Finance and Big Whatever Else. Meanwhile, Republicans charge the Democrats are in bed with Big Unions and Big Education. What few have pointed out is that they all, every last one of them regardless of party, are motivated to follow the direction of some special interest and that is precisely why the Senate was created the way that it was, to be a check on that type of activity. Nowadays, the Senate is nothing more than an elitist version of the House. Again, remember friends that the Senate is not now called the Millionaire's club for nothing.

Rarely do I find myself agreeing with filmmaker/agitator Michael Moore, yet on the following point I must agree wholeheartedly. Moore wrote once that everyone knows that it is lobbyists that conduct the research, generate the position papers and ultimately write the legislation. According to Moore, perhaps we should just let the lobbyists vote and eliminate the middleman. It is a sad punch line to repeat, but one that is ultimately on the mark.

Naturally, money is never going to be expunged from the political process. There are already rules and regulations in place that politicians routinely ignore. When they are caught, the politicians simply pay the ethics fine as if it were nothing more than the cost of doing business.

As we have seen with the Blagojevich corruption saga in Illinois, corruption will continue to taint the process even if the 17th Amendment is abolished. However, if a Senator were hired by the legislature of his or her state, then he or she would be subject to either recall or replacement for unethical behavior. Rather than run around the state raising money for six years to secure yet another term, the job of the Senator will simply be to go to Washington and be a part of that deliberative body that maintains an important check on the whims of the people at large.

Answering to the state legislatures might mean Senators would find the incentive to actually read the legislation written by the lobbyists before they cast their vote. Now, imagine the efficiency such a requirement might produce.

The original Senate was designed to be a check on the House of Representatives and, hence, a check on the people who voted those Representatives to office. In Federalist Paper Number 63, James Madison writes that the Senate is supposed to be a "defense to the people against their own temporary errors and delusions."

Yes, indeed, government By The People and the theories that led to the U.S. Constitution state that even the people themselves can become tyrannical. When the people demand that a segment of the population living in this country illegally be given the same rights as those here legally, that is tyranny. In that instance, those people living here illegally are given the opposite of exactly what caused the American Revolution: representation without taxation.

When an individual's disposable income is derived almost solely through the government, by way of Section 8 housing, WIC, food stamps, and Medicaid, and that individual pays no taxes - even though they are an able-bodied and able-minded adult - then they receive "representation without taxation." As my colleague who coined the phrase, conservative commentator Austin Rhodes contends that representation without taxation is every bit as tyrannical as it's opposite. The people who get the perks continue on to tyranny by voting based solely on what the politicians will continue to give them individually and not to the public at large. These people know the politicians will give them anything they want if they continue to take caravans of voters to the polls. And these people are represented by hordes of lobbyists who get rich by promising the poor more perks. The fact that someone else is forced to pay for all that free stuff others get is tyranny perpetrated.

As long as the moochers get to vote for members of both houses of the legislature and their lobbyists wield the same influence in both houses the tyranny will continue. If the Senate operated as it was intended to, welfare rolls would decrease because the states would be in a position to curb the problem. States with low unemployment would band together and demand their citizens no longer pay for other state's moochers.

Republicans love to call themselves the party of fiscal conservatism, but it was a Democrat president who began welfare reform under the gun of Congressional conservatives. The public assistance nightmare the country faces is the subject of chapter 4, but it should suffice to say that Senators beholden to the states - and not the tyrannical masses enjoying their representation without taxation - would be more apt to reign in the very things that crush state governments. True welfare reform would be at the top of the to-do list.

Each and every state in this union is different on many different levels. Some states are better suited to agriculture and others to heavy industry. There are states that rely almost solely on tourism and others that haven't seen a tourist in decades. Issues pertaining to states are different as well. Arizona has a problem with illegal immigration whereas Rhode Island does not. Water availability is among the biggest issues facing Georgians, but the good people of Michigan will never have that issue as long as Lake Michigan does not dry up and turn to desert. I certainly do not think that will happen in our lifetimes. Well, Global Warming could turn it into a desert, but I digress.

Some states are poorer than others. I cannot afford to live in Connecticut, but I live quite comfortably in Georgia. Some states need coal power to survive, others depend more on nuclear power or natural gas. The cost of heating a home in South Carolina is far different from that of North Dakota or New York. South Carolina has never had a lake effect snowstorm and the average Dakotan does not fear hurricanes. People in Florida are, as a state, older by average than the people in Idaho, so health care might be more of an issue to Floridians than people in the potato state.

Therein lays the beauty of the 10th Amendment. As it states, power not expressly given to federal government belongs to the states or to the people (through the use of amendments). That mean Georgia needs to deal with her water issues and Arizona needs to enforce her borders. In cases of state versus state disagreements, border patrol, education, and many other issues, the states might need to, and are allowed to under the Constitution, request the assistance of the federal government.

According to the Constitution and the 10th Amendment, this does not work the other way around. The federal government has no business telling Georgia how it will house its poor; the Constitution forbids it by not expressly giving the national government that power.

The federal government has no business telling Hawaii it must follow the same health care guidelines as Florida. The Constitution forbids it by not giving the feds power to regulate health coverage within the borders of a state. In 1789, if the Framers believed everyone had the right to a good bloodletting, they would have allowed for a universal health system and made health care a right.

The Constitution forbids the federal government from telling North Carolina it must allow abortions; and if California wants to be the "partial birth abortion state," so be it. Abortion has nothing to do with interstate commerce or the general welfare. If the People feel the rights of the unborn should be addressed, it requires a Constitutional amendment, not a Supreme Court ruling. Without an amendment, it is a state issue, pure and simple.

I have already illustrated how the People sometimes can make hideous decisions at the voting booth by casting a ballot for people based on what they personally will get as opposed to what is good for the nation or just because they personally like the sound of a candidate's name. Yet for the sake of this discussion, I feel it is relevant in talking about the deliberation of the Senate to expand on our friends in South Carolina and their stellar Democratic Party Senate candidate.

You remember that Democrat voters in the Palmetto State went to the polls in 2010 and nominated a man who was unemployed, lived with his father and had pending criminal sex charges against him as their candidate for the U.S. Senate. This man, Alvin Greene, did not campaign, did not raise money, had no campaign materials and did not once deliver a speech longer than seven minutes to a crowd of supporters.

After winning the primary, Greene was faced with television cameras and he looked like a deer caught in headlights. He responded to questions with one-word answers. Rather than cite any issue, his answer as to why he decided to run was something along the lines of 'I've always wanted to.'

Yeah, Al Greene would certainly add to the deliberate nature of the Senate. That is, if the Senate wants to descend into deliberate idiocy. His first actual speech lasted just seven minutes and was so short on any specifics even the perfectly handpicked crowd of potential supporters at an NAACP meeting in his hometown walked away shaking their heads. Even the very folks who will admit to for voting for candidates based on their skin color realized this guy was beyond slow when it came to discussing the issues he would encounter as a U.S. Senator. His assertions about education reform came across as almost being functionally retarded. Yes, I said "retarded."

Aiken County, SC is one of the larger South Carolina political districts in terms of voter awareness and activism. Presidential hopefuls, Democrat and Republican, routinely make stops in the area. The Aiken County Democratic Party thought so little of Alvin Greene that they refused to place Greene's picture on their candidate list web page. They also did not include a proper link to Greene's website as they did with the other candidates. They did, however, provide a link to the man running against Greene; ironically, they backed the candidate of the Green Party.

So, how did Al Greene manage to snag a Senate nomination away from a well-known, well funded, Democrat soldier? It was not a Republican conspiracy, it was voters who were acting almost as retarded as the candidate. Should Alvin Greene have won, he likely would do exactly what all modern Senators do, and that is vote according to the desires of the people who are willing to give them money.

The people of the United States are the most franchised people in the world. Citizens here can vote for county and city council seats, school board trustees, state legislatures, coroners, governors, and in some places dog catcher. Americans can vote in referendums and for sales tax projects. In most states, the voters choose the governor's cabinet. There are 435 seats in the House of Representatives all voted in by the people. The President is not

Elected by a popular vote, nor are the members of the Supreme Court. Neither should members of the Senate be popularly elected.

The first plank of the Contract On The Government is the immediate repeal of the 17th Amendment. This is the first stop on the roadway to reform and don't let the politicians tell you otherwise, the repeal of the 17th Amendment is vital to the survival of the United States.

Chapter 3.
The Executive from Finance to Warfare

George Washington was asked and declined the notion that he should accept the position of king of the newly liberated colonies. It was Washington who also set the precedent of the President only serving two terms. Over the years, the presidency though, did grow from the executive that only signed off on legislation and directed its enforcement through a small bureaucracy to the most powerful political office held in the world with legions on minions that can never be fully controlled by just one living being. The founders knew that tasking one person to control a vast empire and its bureaucracy would, one day, lead to trouble and that is why they shaped the executive branch to allow for growth while keeping some important checks on presidential power.

It was his knowledge and understanding that the Constitutional constraints still were not enough to stop the possibility of a future American Caesar that caused President Washington to impose term limits on himself and his compatriots who served after him followed his example making it almost what you could consider a gentleman's agreement bound by honor. The original presidents might be pleased to have the knowledge that only one man so far has not followed the two-term limit. After Franklin D. Roosevelt's four-term White House streak, the country finally recognized the gentleman's agreement as the supreme law of the land by way of a Constitutional amendment.

While Roosevelt cannot be compared at all with the murderous Hitler, it was during his reign that Americans of Japanese decent were held against their will in concentration camps and Americans of

African descent continued to be terrorized in the South. Hitler himself commented that NAZI Germany had more in common with America than it had differences. Without that important term limit on the Presidency, the eventuality could have easily been an American Hitler. Remember, Hitler made it into office by totally legal means. He also became a despot and mass murderer legally.

Even with the term limits in place, the presidency has become an institution unbalanced in size, authority, and concentration of power. Briefly, it is the most powerful political entity in the history of mankind. However, the President is not a sovereign and to keep it that way the office must have checks placed upon it.

The presidency does need to be a strong institution. Generally throughout our nation's history, when presidents have abused their power, the rules of the Constitution have been followed. Of course, there have been some times when Presidents got away with what might have been considered criminal behavior; LBJ's Gulf Of Tonkin and Reagan's Iran Contra are two recent examples. Every modern President has lived under a microscope and still the institution has remained stable despite the incredible growth in domestic as well as world power. Yet, there is a little wobble that has occurred in the institution and caused by two factors.

Over time, the presidency has moved in some ways it should not and been hemmed in other ways by circumstances that could not have reasonably been anticipated by the framers. Those two issues have to do with money and war. The Contract On The Government demands that the President be given broader powers in terms of checking Congressional spending and Congress needs to reform this nations security apparatus to conform to the Constitution and in doing so reign in some serious executive excesses.

Let us start with the current limitations on the executive's fiscal powers and a lack of ability to reign in congressional spending.

The whole idea of adding a rider to a bill started off by necessity due to the technological limitations of the 18th and 19th Centuries. Actually, the folks around then did not realize they were technologically limited, but compared with us, they were. In that time before the jet airplane, a Representative might have learned of a problem in his state that needed direct federal attention but found there was little time to act hence the federal earmark or rider.   For example, he might learn the federally built lock and dam on the Savannah River is failing and the states of South Carolina and Georgia need help in repairing it immediately. Since the lock and dam is used for interstate commerce, then the government needs to act. So rather than wait for a bill having to do with waterways and barge commerce to come up in session, or write a totally new bill that has to wind its way through committee, the representative simply asks it be added as a rider to a clean air bill already under consideration.

Riders are supposed to be a tool when time is of the essence and that was important in the horse and buggy days because you would not want to wait months for the appropriate committee to convene when you need a dam fix now. What has happened though is that riders of all shapes and sizes appear in almost every bill passed and it is through this "pork" that billions and billions of dollars are wasted every year.

One of my favorite political cartoons ever was drawn by artist Rick McKee of the Augusta Chronicle. The panel shows a highway with an overpass, a building and trees and shrubs with signs posted everywhere. The signs read: the Robert C. Bird Memorial Highway, the Robert C. Byrd Overpass, the Robert C. Byrd Welcome Center, the Robert C. Byrd Bush, the Robert C. Byrd Tree and, the punch line, the Robert C. Byrd "Bird." I found that hilarious, sort of.

Politicians know that bringing home the pork brings them the votes. Yes, people love to see road signs on the highway announcing the Robert C. Byrd Memorial Parkway because that highway was necessary, but do the people need a $35 million dollar James E. Clyburn Transportation Center at the South Carolina State University?

The latter controversial project has undergone years worth of audits because a healthy (or unhealthy) amount of the money allocated for the project cannot as of this writing be accounted for and it has taken a decade to date to break ground on the actual building. If you think that is an exaggeration, then look for yourself at the hideous amount of money spent each year on stupid vanity projects across the country meant only to excite and expand a particular politicians voting base. Indeed, Mr. James Clyburn is only one member of Congress and yet according to a 2010 compilation of pork by the group Citizens Against Public Waste, Clyburn has been able to rack up $55 million dollars in earmarks. Shouldn't the President have some say on things like this before he signs the bill?

While studying possible corruption with redevelopment of blighted areas of my city, I came across a $1 million dollar earmark, or rider, given to a group called the East Augusta Development Corporation. The money had been inserted into a transportation bill sponsored by Democrat Representative John Barrow.

What is interesting is that East Augusta Development Corp. is not a government body; it is a Community Housing Development Corporation (or commonly called a CHoDO). These private groups ostensibly go into blighted areas, demolish the blight, and create affordable new housing. The problem is once the money is earmarked to them, there is no way to determine if they use it for the intended purpose or if they put it on a salad plate and eat it for supper. To date, I have been unable to verify that the East Augusta Development Corp. has ever demolished a slum or built a new house. This particular CHoDO was created by a local city commissioner and appears to be nothing other than a pile of paperwork. Furthermore, groups such as East Augusta Development Corp. already get funding from the state and local governments (I will expand on that in the bureaucracy chapter), so why is such a thing necessary to be placed in a transportation bill?

The answer to that is simple, the voting bloc that lives in the district that the East Augusta Development Corp. serves, commonly called the Laney Walker District, is run by a group of politicos that are very effective in delivering votes on election day. How does it hurt John Barrow to sneak them a million dollars as his pet charity if it snags him some votes? They get a million dollars on the promise that church vans will be rolling on Election Day. And so what if the pet charity doesn't use the money wisely, that is not Barrow's problem. All that matters is that he has secured his votes. This is why the President needs to be given line item review and line veto power on any bill that requires spending.

Everyone remembers the money spent to research cow farts, but that study is by far not the most outrageous. Here is a quick look at fun projects over the years that you, the tax payer, funded:

The Buffalo Bill Museum

The Montana Sheep Institute

Brown Tree Snake Control in Guam

The Sparta Teapot Museum

The Center For Grape Genetics

Communication with Extra-Terrestrials

Study on Wood Utilization

The Commercial Kitchen Business Incubator

Monroe County, KY Farmers Market

Myrtle Beach, SC Convention Center

The Robert C. Byrd Institute (no joke!)

The Charles Rangel Center for Public Service

Paint Shield for Protecting People from Microbial Threats

There may be some valid reason out there to map the genome of grapes, but can someone explain to me what the heck a commercial kitchen business incubator is or what it does? And doesn't Myrtle Beach have enough income from tourists to afford to build a conference center?

The amount of money wasted on earmarks is absolutely mindless, but there are people out there that actually defend the practice. Earmarks, they say, stimulate the economy by investing in infrastructure. Sorry, "hey, honey, for vacation this year why don't we drive to North Carolina and take the kids to the Sparta Teapot Museum," said no one ever.

Defenders also say even if every dime from every earmark were yanked that it still wouldn't make a dent in paying down the national debt. Now what kind of logic is that? And you will find that twisted thesis applied to every area of fiscal negligence that is highlighted in this book. Simply remove the word earmark from the first sentence in this paragraph and replace it with welfare or foreign aid. So it makes good sense that since we already owe a gazillion dollars in debt that we can't pay down, then we might as well spend a gazillion more studying how to use wood, giving cell phones to welfare brood mares and arming our enemies! Sorry, but that rationale is simply fucked up.

A line item veto would go a long way to solving the earmark problem, but the Congress cannot give that power to the President for one simple reason: they are not empowered to expand Presidential veto power. Notice I did not say 'legislative' power. That is because an expansion of the President's veto authority does not mean he is crafting legislation. A line item veto on riders and earmarks pursuant to congressional spending means the President simply has the power to cut out wasteful spending that has no bearing to the function of the bill presented for his signature. Another reason you do not want the Congress attempting to give this authority to the President is because the next Congress can simply revoke it if they are of the opposing party. History records that situation has already occurred. The line item veto needs to be bestowed in the manner of an amendment to the Constitution.

Allowing the Congress to "discontinue" the earmark practice is not enough either for the same reason listed above. When enough votes are present, the Congress can simply repeal its former repeal of riders. Naturally, they would do it on a Friday night in November when no one is watching, listening, or reading the news.

Such an amendment would do nothing except clarify that the President may veto the "extra" fiscal related portions of a bill he or she deems are unnecessary to the enforcement of the overall bill.

What happens currently is that the President will receive a much-needed funding bill for troops overseas. Buried in that bill will be millions if not billions in unnecessary spending for things that have nothing to do with feeding and arming the military. The President can either sign the bill in total, or veto the bill in total. He cannot veto out the so-called pork. It is here that the President is tied over a barrel because a full veto will force the bill to go back to Congress for another stalling session that delays the needed funding. The President also gets the double humiliation of being tarred and feathered as being against American soldiers for vetoing sending them food rations. A simple sentence in the amendment I propose through the Contract would take care of that little problem and save the treasury billions of dollars each year. It would save the treasury not millions, mind you, but billions…with a B.

Opponents of the line item veto point out the President could use the tool for retribution. He or she could reward Georgia with the Thomas Scott Hudson Laboratory for the Study of Facial Recognition in Advanced Reptile Species, but decline much needed funding for a cancer center in Massachusetts simply because one Congressional group supported him on a matter and the other did not or he could give preferential treatment of members of his own party. The way that dilemma is solved is the veto override, which is a power Congress already has in their toolkit.

Another Congressional check on the President's line item veto power would be for the Congress to simply craft a separate bill if that cancer center is so important and simply use earmarks for what they were intended for in the first place: emergency spending.

Also, if a comprehensive list of all earmarks was published indicating which ones were allowed and which were line-item vetoed, journalists would gleefully report on presidential abuse of the power if it occurred. In fact, giving the press something to do other than reporting the latest antics of Lady Gaga would help the struggling newspaper industry and create jobs by giving people in the media more stacks of data to research. The lucky byproduct would also be that we might see less of Gaga's mug splashed everywhere, but again,

I digress.

The bottom line is a scalpel on the earmarks would save every tax-payer in this country untold amounts of money. After a time, it might just so happen that the Clyburns of the world might think twice before adding in useless pork if they know their initiative will be publicly vetoed. In the scientific world, they call this the Hawthorne effect. That is, subjects that are aware they are being studied tend to change their behavior if they believe they might suffer humiliation or any other adverse affect due to their actions.

The President needs expanded power in the financial area, but the office also needs to be forced to follow the Constitution when it comes to warfare and intelligence gathering. This important plank of the Contract On The Government would save the treasury billions and more importantly, it will save scores of American lives. The President must be required to follow the Constitution when it comes to the provision on war and other activities related to warfare. One point on which George Washington was clear was that warfare would continue in perpetuity if a military industrial complex combined with a large standing army were allowed to co-exist. We have that in America today.

On the issue of warfare the Constitution is clear, the Congress declares war and the President is the Commander In Chief of the armed forces. It is important to note that the last war that was officially declared by Congress were the declarations written against Germany and Japan in 1941.

Korea, The Bay of Pigs, Vietnam, Grenada, Panama, Operation Desert Storm, Kosovo, the War on Terror in Afghanistan and Iraq, and all other warlike engagements since World War II were all either undeclared or simply called "police actions" or "conflicts." Constitutionally, the problem with the War Powers Act, or WPA, that currently stands as law is that, again, Congress cannot vote to limit a President's executive duties and the language defining war is vague in the Constitution other than the supreme phrase that gives the Congress the power to declare war.

In the years since the WPA was made law, Presidents have generally respected it but they are not necessarily required to and that is why we have conflicts and not wars. The matter has never been the subject of a Supreme Court review and neither the executive nor legislative branches want a showdown in the judicial venue, so neither has pressed the matter.

George Washington warned back in his day about standing armies and hinted at a military industrial complex long before President Dwight Eisenhower uttered that phrase. Indeed, Washington's warning came long before the word industrial meant what it does today. What Washington may not have foreseen were submarines, night vision goggles, satellites and all the gadgets of the modern world and how the world would eventually turn into a place where America would almost constantly be at war. Wait, during his time European countries had been at war with each other for centuries, so maybe he did look into the future and that is why he warned against a military industrial complex!

In conflict, the Congress can either cut off the money which would strand troops overseas, or they can let the President run roughshod should he choose to; and we know the latter has happened all too often. The provisions in the WPA, though, are reasonable. If the country or its interests are attacked, the President can act swiftly. However, when it is a situation like Iraq, more deliberation is necessary before the government commits the armed forces to a prolonged engagement and occupation of foreign soil. Remember, almost every major war fought with the exception of World War II for the past two centuries was thought would happen and end quickly and none ever have. It takes more than shock and awe to conquer a people. Therefore, it should take more than a Presidential decree to commit our armed forces to the battlefield.

It is sour to me that Teddy Roosevelt is hailed as a progressive reformer and William Howard Taft is known only for being so fat that he once got himself stuck in the White House bathtub, which actually never happened. Taft very publicly said he would follow the Constitution as he rolled back some of excesses of the Roosevelt administration. Taft also noted the need for a strong military for the defense of the nation, but rejected aggressive warfare. He was not interested in inserting himself into Europe's problems and meticulously adhered to his Constitutional duties. This enraged Roosevelt, who then ran against his former friend for the Presidency.

Thanks to Roosevelt, the 1912 election ushered in Woodrow Wilson who went on to use the Constitution so much as toilet paper. Under Wilson, America interfered in World War I, Americans of German decent were placed in concentration camps, Americans of African descent were lynched in the South, and the Committee on Public Information was created. Historians now admit that the CPI was nothing less than the blueprint for Hitler's Propaganda Ministry.

Wilson was indeed one of the architects of the Versailles Treaty that crushed Germany financially and created the atmosphere that allowed for the rise of Hitler. Speaking of the mentoring of Adolf Hitler, Wilson's domestic piece de resistance was the creation of the Sedition Act, which made it illegal for a citizen to exercise their 1st Amendment right and criticize the government in a time of war. Now how progressive is that?

The historic record is clear that Wilson wanted war in his first term of office even as he campaigned for a second term on the slogan "he kept us out of war." His continued meddling in European affairs not only eventually helped create World War II; it set the precedent for American involvement in one foreign policy disaster after another.

The War Powers Act must be inserted into the Constitution and the language already there enforced with the demand that a declaration of war be issued by Congress before troops are committed to anything other than an emergency defense of this country's borders or vital assets.

In such a case such as the conflict in Iraq and the almost assured future action in Iran, the President would need a little more than some fuzzy satellite photos to wage a years-long, expensive campaign. Allowing for the President's emergency action powers combined with some accountability will force restraint on the government as a whole. If Iraq's Saddam Hussein needed to be toppled from power so badly while a war theatre was still hot in Afghanistan, then under the Constitution, a declaration of war against Iraq needed to be proclaimed. Sidestepping the issue by saying no one was at war with Iraq, but at war against terror is stupid and ridiculous. Terror is an emotion, only the psychotic go to war with their emotions and that too generally results in innocent people being hurt.

Countries go to war against countries, not words. The very idea of a War on Terror was nothing more than the continuation of a disastrous foreign policy built around a slogan sold to the American people with Paul McCartney warbling onstage setting the groundwork for a wave of patriotism that would diminish as quickly as it crested. Once we determined Osama Bin Laden was training mercenaries and living as a guest in Afghanistan, the President should have offered an ultimatum to the (unrecognized) Taliban regime and then asked the Congress for a declaration of war, not against terror, but against Afghanistan. A country that had no real central government, was being run by fanatical warlords who trained and hosted men who killed 3000 people on American soil and acknowledged it was harboring the criminal mastermind behind the 9/11 attacks deserved to be invaded by way of a declaration from the Congress. To do anything otherwise is to take away legitimacy of the war effort both at home and in the international community. To do otherwise is to mar the memory of the patriots that gave their life the day America was attacked by her own airplanes.

People are far more patriotic and willing ride the thing out if they understand the country is involved in a declared fighting war rather than a "conflict." It must be noted that we really had no choice but to eventually invade both Afghanistan and Iraq, that lot had been cast decades before New York and Washington were ever attacked. I attempted to join the Army during the time because I understood our country was at peril due to circumstances that began to evolve decades before I was born. In my own naïveté, I failed to realize my patriotism was causing me to want to put on a uniform to serve the very political regime that had in part caused the attacks by way of its years of meddling in other country's affairs.

You might say that the above language is acting as a Monday morning quarterback, but not so, what I am saying is simply follow the Constitution in matters of foreign policy and warfare and you get more deliberation, not hare-brained schemes like Vietnam and the grandfather of blunders the Bay of Pigs. For those of you not up on history, the Bay of Pigs was an operation devised by a secretive Cold War creation called the Central Intelligence Agency. Intelligence gathering was once under the control of the Army as the Office of Strategic Services until some wise group, namely Congress, decided to make it its own stand-alone agency. Over a short time it grew into a separate and secretive paramilitary force and now it routinely gets the United States into trouble. In the early 1960's the CIA trained and funded Cuban exiles in an attempt to invade the island and the U.S. military was to provide air support.

The attack didn't go so well. Fidel Castro may be a communist despot, but he is no fool. Reason suggests that someone should have seen at the time that the CIA was operating outside the bounds of the Constitution. Since the death of President Kennedy, numerous conspiracy theories have abounded around the Dealey Plaza assassination and they all point to some CIA involvement in the assassination. Rather than get into the theories or develop yet another here, it is reasonable to say that having a large bureaucracy of civilians acting in a military capacity with no real oversight is clearly not something the Framers would have wanted included in national government.

The mere fact that it is illegal to out the name of a CIA "civilian" employee should scare the public.

A country needs spies and there was plenty of espionage practiced in the Revolution and every other American engagement before the advent of the CIA. But rather than have a healthy espionage apparatus under the control of military generals, at this point the CIA is part of a broader group called the Intelligence Community commonly known as the IC. This conglomerate is comprised of 16 separate agencies that look into everything from drug smuggling to foreign affairs. They all brief the President; but history shows that on many occasions the President either wasn't briefed fully in a matter, wasn't briefed at all, was briefed with erroneous information or was himself complicit in CIA activities that were clearly illegal. Does anyone remember the Gulf of Tonkin affair?

Anyone who understands geopolitical paradigms can see the clear process that led to our current conflicts in the Middle East. The process began with the CIA, apparently under the direction of President Eisenhower, using almost Soviet styled tactics to overthrow the democratically elected government in Iran. They installed the dictator of their choice, the Shah, and later Americans stood back in disbelief and rage when the Islamic Revolution occurred decades later in that country.

I can still remember all the yellow ribbons during the hostage crisis, my emotions were filled with hate for the bearded zealots not understanding the Islamic Revolution itself was about removing America's hand-picked despot. What the Iranians did not realize was that they were trading in one totalitarian regime for one just as evil. Rather than learn from their mistakes, the CIA then decided to arm and support Saddam Hussein of Iraq against the new Iranian regime.

Hussein was goaded into war with Iran and naturally (and rightfully so) the Iranians blamed America. The propaganda of Israel being the real reason radical Islam was created is largely just that, propaganda and myth. Certainly, America's support of the Jewish state has been a major cause for controversy in the Arab world, but it was the United Nations and not America that set up the state of Israel. America along with everyone else simply recognized her. Revisionist history wants to paint America as an empire that marched into Palestine and gave it to the Israelis. Not so, Palestine was under direct control of the sovereign crown of the United Kingdom, therefore, it was technically theirs to give to anyone of their choosing.

The beginnings of the "war on terror" began with America's meddling in the affairs of independent sovereign countries like Iran, Afghanistan, Iraq, Northern Yemen and Saudi Arabia. What made the invasion of Afghanistan in 2001 so difficult was another product of CIA meddling decades before. When the Soviet armies invaded that country in 1979, the CIA armed to the hilt a "freedom fighter" group that was known at the time as the Mujahideen and armed and funded a young Saudi, Osama Bin Laden as well.   After the disaster in Iran, the CIA did not want the Soviets to occupy the country of Afghanistan, which has large natural gas reserves and shares a border with enemy Iran. Again, in what looked like a profitable yet dangerous game for both the CIA and the American arms industry, no one at the time took any note that not one single army had managed invade, occupy and hang on to Afghanistan since Genghis Khan achieved the feat in the 13th century, and even he did not keep the territory for very long.

The Soviets were bound to lose their Afghan adventure without America's involvement. Years later, after the Soviets gave up and left, the Mujahedeen morphed into the Taliban and Bin Laden created Al Qaeda. American suddenly went from friend to the freedom fighters to enemy of the terrorists. That would never have happened had we left them alone in the first place and simply stood back and snickered watching the Soviets getting their tails burned.

Congress has tried in piecemeal fashion to reign in its little pet demon. After the 9/11 attacks, Congress agreed to fund equipment and operations but not a massive increase in staff. The CIA, again in all their abounding wisdom, simply circumvented Congress and used the funding to hire mercenaries cloaking them under the term of 'outsourcing.' What you are reading is correct. Groups such as Blackwater are really private mercenary companies hired by the CIA.

A full 70% of the US intelligence budget went to the hiring of mercenaries and other groups providing administrative assistance according to investigative journalist Tim Shorrock in his book Spies For Hire.

Do these mercenary groups torture people? They certainly have been accused of it, but we don't know. Does the CIA know if torture has been outsourced? We don't know because they have this thing called plausible deniability. Do these mercenary groups assassinate people? We don't know and again, the CIA has plausible deniability. How many of these groups exist? We don't know and the CIA is not telling. Do they operate inside the United States? They are not supposed to, but the simple fact is that we do not know.

The IC has grown so large and so complicated that entire books of research are devoted to attempting to flesh out what the IC actually does and how large an operation it is. But since they are apparently not subject to the Freedom Of Information Act, they do not have to tell us. They maintain that they are there to provide for national security and to protect our freedoms, but there is really no mechanism for oversight that can prove they are doing what they say they are doing. More importantly, there is no oversight to prove they are not doing what they could be doing, and that fact is scary.

Even critics of the information presented here must agree that the CIA is a secretive paramilitary organization; it is a militia. The US Constitution provides the states may have civilian militias and the federal government a standing army and navy. Nowhere does it say the executive branch or the legislative branch may have its own civilian militia. Naturally, people will want to say the CIA is an 'intelligence-gathering organization' but they cannot deny the CIA is armed and that makes them an armed civilian militia of the federal government. The NAZI German Schutzstaffel, was a secretive paramilitary force made up chiefly of non-military personnel that operated largely outside of legitimate German borders and they hired mercenaries too. History knows the Schutzstaffel as the dreaded SS.

No matter the intentions in creating the IC, there is no check and no balance on the CIA and its 15 other sister organizations. To avoid the painful lessons of the past, there absolutely must be some accountability. Noted Blackwater researcher Jeffery Scahill briefly examines the biggest problem with hiring mercenaries, in a piece written for The Nation. Schill quotes Robert Grenier who is a former top official in the CIA's counter-terrorism unit as saying "I can assure you that if the CIA were employing a contractor who had, thereby, access to very sensitive information, [the CIA] would take a very dim view of that same individual working for that company under a different contract, say, for the Israelis or for some other foreign government." Grenier's quote is putting it lightly. No, we do not want them contracting with any foreign power if they know this country's sensitive secrets!

The Romans hired mercenaries to protect their frontier borders. Eventually, the mercenaries demanded more money and Rome refused, so the mercenaries turned on Rome. While the sacking of Rome by people once paid to protect it did not in and of itself spell the end of the Roman Empire, it set it on the wane and ushered in what many call the Dark Ages. There were no more technical triumphs, there was no more battlefield glory, and eventually there was no more Roman Empire. On this subject, we can turn to the words of another renowned political thinker of old. Niccolo Machiavelli wrote in The Prince, "And if the first disaster to the Roman Empire should be examined, it will be found to have commenced only with the enlisting of the Goths; because from that time the vigor of the Roman Empire began to decline, and all that valor which had raised it passed away to others."

The CIA should have learned the lesson from the Mujahedeen that arming any group who has not taken an oath to the flag of the United States is a dangerous and unstable move. As Scahill reports, his source Grenier admits the outsourcing organizations, or private mercenary groups, are already practicing a form of collective bargaining. The war is not even over and they are already asking for more money. They know our secrets too and one day those secrets will be up to the highest bidder. The intelligence "business" is a vast and unknown organization and it must be, over a period of time, folded back to where it constitutionally belongs and that is in the United States military.

Whether it is the CIA or the private groups providing intelligence to the office that can constitutionally mass the nation's troops, they have all proven themselves ineffective and prone to delivering erroneous information. That fact alone makes the IC dangerous to the union. Communication between the 16 separate agencies remains weak and the creation of Homeland Security has done little to improve the communication. In fact, Homeland Security has been just another bureaucracy that hasn't lived up to its mission since its inception. In an effort to increase communication between all the various agencies, the Bush administration and Congress simply added more mouths to the trough. As we have seen in the past, all the mouths at the trough continue to be too busy chewing slop to utter a word to one another.

Another element of the IC is the National Security Agency - or the No Such Agency, if you are a government agent. I can attest to you that the NSA does exist and they have a large complex operating at Fort Gordon here in my town of Augusta. One reason the government wants Americans to ignore the NSA is because the NSA is spying on Americans! Murfee Faulk, a former colleague of mine in the media and a former NSA analyst, is on the record stating he was directed to listen in on telephone calls between American citizens. In a recent documentary, Faulk and another colleague confirm they listened to private conversations that had absolutely nothing to do with national security.

Any American who believes it is necessary and proper for the government to eavesdrop on everyday citizens has a warped understanding of this country's laws. Some might believe that if one is doing nothing wrong, then one should not have a problem should a government agent listening in while checking out what is being said on a particular cell phone frequency. That line of thinking is rubbish. What it really means is that I might find myself on a terror watch list for calling my wife at work and telling her to hurry home when she gets off because, "I am going to RIDE you like a 747 and BLOW UP my PACKAGE inside your TEMPLE!"

Surely I jest, right? Wrong, that is exactly the nature of the conversations that former government employee Faulk and his colleagues claim they heard while working for the NSA. So, yes, your sweet nothings may not be as private as you may think. What began in a tiny little office in the 1940's has mushroomed into a vast organization that considers nothing but its own survival to be sacred. The President is no longer in control of the IC any more than he is in control of the daily weather.

Murfee Faulk divulged the phone tapping information years ago and the public yawned. Now, on the heels of the scandal involving the IRS targeting certain groups for audits while ordering porn and pizza on government credit cards and attending conferences that include line dancing and Star Trek reenactments, along comes Edward Snowden reinforcing what we already know about the NSA and CIA. The big difference between Faulk and Snowden is that Faulk did not feel it necessary to steal government documents to prove his story. Faulk also did not fly off to a communist country's territory and start spilling secrets that had nothing to do with our country's domestic spying.

The Snowden saga cements two of the important points of this chapter: Yes this government spies on its own citizens and employs mercenaries they call "contractors" to do the work. With Snowden we see how dangerous it is to subcontract intelligence work as he has proven he is no more loyal to the United States than is the President of Russia.

As noted earlier, President Eisenhower knew what was coming when he gave his televised farewell address in 1960. Eisenhower knew the CIA was planning the Bay of Pigs and American arms manufacturers were in the middle of the scheme as well. The address of

Eisenhower's is eerily familiar to Washington's farewell in that it warned of large standing armies. Still, what Eisenhower warned of was something Washington would have a hard time comprehending, a real military industrial complex. Unlike a standing army, a MIC profits off the sales of arms, the proliferation of conflict, and the loss of life. The MIC is not concerned who is in the right, who is the freedom fighter and who is the terrorist; they are only concerned with selling their wares. The MIC's wares kill people.

The Military Industrial Complex predates Eisenhower. The carnage of World War I was going to be ugly no matter what, but it was made uglier by American secret weapons sales to the Europeans.

The steamship Lusitania and almost every other ship of the time that sailed out of American ports into the Atlantic carried arms overseas. America provided the mustard and chlorine gases along with all the bullets needed to prolong the conflict. In those days of 1915-1916, the Great Peacemaker Woodrow Wilson strutted around the country under a banner of him keeping America out of war knowing full well his administration was allowing stateside arms merchants to profit over the conflict in Europe. It is not possible to arm one side of a war and call yourself neutral. Sure enough, American blood ended having to be spilled before it was all said and done.

The US Military is one of the most efficient organizations on Earth and I would sleep better at night knowing spies are working for the military and not an unconstitutional secretive agency that reports to no one other than arms dealers. After all, if a civilian mercenary turns on the United States, they find themselves charged in a civilian court. But for a member of the military to do so, the charge of treason carries an almost certain death penalty. The military also knows what it needs to carry on its affairs and we need make sure the military is prepared to defend the nation without allowing the MIC to dictate where the next war will be so they can make a profit. The only way to shrink the MIC and the IC and the CIA and the NSA is to place all security and intelligence gathering back in the hands where it belongs: The U.S. military.

The President absolutely must adhere to the Constitution in matters of war, and that means all matters of war. A part of the Contract On the Government must be the demand from the people and states that the President do so, and the template is the War Powers Act. However, again, it is not up to the Congress to attempt to legislate what they think might have been the Framers intent. Make the War Powers Act a portion of the Constitutional amendment that is being suggested as part of the overall Contract.

On the issues of the CIA and the MIC, it will take years to dismantle the current structure and have it moved under the direction of the military without compromising our nation's security. Conventional wisdom says it is impossible. But remember, conventional wisdom in 1776 said a war with England could not be won. Conventional wisdom also said World War I would only last a couple of months and it lasted for years. Conventional wisdom says analysts belonging to the NSA would never sit around and masturbate while secretly listening to other peoples phone sex conversations, but they have…they 'fessed up to it!

Warfare has changed dramatically over the past two centuries and no one should suggest that America's ability to gather information and fight enemies of the country should be diminished. Yet time and history have proven that unchecked and secretive actions by the executive branch and its many agencies simply keep this country in a state of conflict and quagmire, all so that someone can make a buck. The Constitution attempts to limit the President's war making powers, but we have already moved to the place George Washington feared in terms of the treasury being used for massive standing armies and an arms manufacturing industry.

In terms of executive financial control, the communications methods have also changed dramatically over the years and so has the amount of money that winds its way through Washington DC. Rare is the need for emergency powers in the form of attaching riders to bills and the President needs the tools to put an end to this money drain. This along with the other provisions in the Contract will replenish the treasury within a matter of years, not decades.

Those two issues pertaining to the Executive Branch are the 2nd and 3rd planks of the Contract On The Government; one requires amendment language instituting a presidential line item veto and codifying the War Powers Act into the Constitution and the other a simple act of Congress finally reigning in America's secret and unconstitutional arms and intelligence industries. Oops, did I say "simple" and "act of Congress" in the same sentence?

Chapter 4.
The Madness of Lifelong Public Assistance

L ike many Americans, when I graduated from high school, I really saw no reason to go to college. Generally speaking, a diploma is useless for most radio broadcasters. However, by the time I reached the ripe old age of 30, it became clear that I was not going to advance any further without a college degree of some kind. Years before, I had left the world of the disc jockey and worked as a junior sales and marketing executive with a hotel marketing firm. During those years I made some great money, but a little thing called the Internet came along and the world of hotel marketing changed. Hoteliers had Priceline and Expedia and they no longer needed me.

So, in 2000, I entered into the halls of the Georgia university system prepared to be educated and re-enter the workforce with a degree under my belt. It is ironic to me that I went to college with the intentions of following the career path of two of my siblings: the legal field. Yet, when I graduated, I found myself back where I started, standing in front of a microphone instead of a judge. This time, though, the pre-law degree I earned really helped me in my position as a news reporter. Unlike my colleagues in the news business, I was not an English or journalism major. In fact, I only took one class the entire time that had anything to do with journalism and it was a law class titled "media law and ethics." The politicians and elected class in the city of Augusta soon learned a law student with a microphone and an audience is a dangerous thing.

Yes, a guy who sits on the porcelain throne in his house and reads Supreme Court opinions, rather than a collection of Garfield cartoons, is not the same guy you want covering you if you are running a corrupt government. School board attorneys and attorneys for the various other boards and authorities in Augusta learned very quickly that sending a polite letter filled with legalese rejecting my Freedom of Information Act requests would only land me in their office holding a copy of the statute demanding they open every file cabinet in the building. They learned quickly that I was not baffled by their bullshit. So, for me, getting the degree was a soaring career move.

The college experience not only taught me how to understand government and the law, it taught me things about life that most professionals in their early 30's do not get a chance to witness. Since I was not some wet-eared kid living on a trust fund, I had to work and pay for my needs while I attended school. Restaurant jobs offer flexible employment for people attending college, and I found that my time working in restaurants was every bit as informative and enlightening as what I was taught in the college classroom.

Waiting tables is absolutely a course in sociology, you get to meet, greet and discover all types of people. With some of those types you want to spit in their food and send them on their non-tipping-assways, but that is a story for another time. Inside the restaurant there are people who work there for fun, for some it is a second job and for others it is a career. Inside the fishbowl of the cookeries, I really did come across just about every type of individual imaginable.

It was my friendship with a guy we will call "Cedrick" that enlightened me to how a large segment of our society lives. Cedrick was the dishwasher for the restaurant. A pit bull build of a man, Cedrick looked either like the guy you would not want to encounter in a dark alley or the guy you took into a dark alley with you for protection. He weighed at least 250 lbs. and had a mouth full of gold teeth. No one in the restaurant found it odd that Cedrick drove a near brand new Cadillac on a dishwasher's salary. It wasn't odd because Cedrick was also the guy you went to procure whatever recreational drug you happened to prefer. Coke, meth, pot, pills – whatever you needed – Cedrick was your man.

If his stature was not intimidating enough, he had a large tattoo on his arm that said "slapaho." I asked him one time about the tat and he said, "that's my tribe, I'm a slap-a-ho." Cute. That tattoo was certainly not going to get him a job as a domestic violence counselor.

Cedrick and I did not start out as buddies, but there was once when his car was in the shop getting "tricked" and he asked me for a ride home after work. I noticed that he stayed in one of our many local housing projects. Now, you may think you know where I am going with this and I will ask you to calmly read on. No, that ride to his home was just a typical ride with me trying to decode his Ebonics into English worried the entire time he might have something in his pocket that could send us both to jail should I make an error and get pulled over in a traffic stop. I didn't think to ask him if he was packing drugs until we were well underway with me driving a nice car in a bad neighborhood. Thankfully, I got him home that night without incident.

It was weeks later after that ride home that Cedrick took a cigarette break outside while I too was taking a break. He dropped his gigantic frame down next to me on the bench out behind the restaurant and lit up a smoke. I always brought a schoolbook with me to work so I could study during the down time at the restaurant. This particular day I had brought my Comparative Politics textbook and I was reading about the European Union.

When Cedrick sat down next to me, he said, "Whatcha readin', dog?"

"Oh," I replied, almost with amusement, "it's really boring stuff, I am reading about the European Union."

Now, most business professionals I encounter to this day have really no idea about what the EU is, who's in it or how it started and that is why what followed was absolutely stunning.

"Actually dog, I like dat shit, and you know I think the UK was right in not going to the Euro, it just ain't time yet."

My mouth was on the pavement and any stereotype in my mind about Cedrick was about to be shattered.

"Yeah," Cedrick continued as if he had been attending the class with me. "I think those mo-fuckers need to look more at the American model. Dey need to go deeper than just a bunch of treaties foe they try to manage dey own currency. You know what I'm sayin'?"

Holy Shit! Here was a dishwashing, drug-dealing thug discussing international political paradigms with me over a Kool cigarette and he knew what he was talking about! He understood a complicated inter-governmental structure that had most of the kids in my college class cramming all night to avoid failing the final.

"Cedrick," I blurted out in shock, "how did you learn all about the Treaty of Nice?"

"Shit, dog," he replied smiling through his gold grill. "This nigga knows how to read."

Cedrick did know how to read, and it was obvious he read voraciously. In our further break time conversations, I learned he had a particular interest in World War II. Most historians have now pretty much reached a consensus that Hitler's fatal move was not Operation Barbarossa, but the failure of Operation Sea Lion. Or as Cedrick put it:

"Dat mo-fucker Hitler didn't have no choice, cuz he knew Stalin would invade him, it was just a matter of time. Hitler knew he had to strike first. No, what fucked him up was not killing England. Dat mo-fucker thought he could win a war with airplanes, you can't win no war with no mo-fuckin' plane, shit. Den, the dumb mu-fucker declared war on us, which he didn't have to do. Dumbest shit I ever seen, you know what I'm sayin'?"

Yep.

As time went on, I tried to explain to Cedrick why he needed to be in college. A man with his mind could go so far in life! But rather, he was living in government housing, working a minimum wage job and selling wares that would eventually either land him in prison or get him killed. His response to me was that he had it great, much better than most people. He made mad money, had plenty of women at his beck and call, bought what he wanted, read what he wanted to read, and yes, it was dangerous, but why trade in his lifestyle when it was so easy?

Cedrick told me how he lived and how he gamed the welfare system and was completely frank about his lifestyle and the lifestyles of other like him. First, one needs a "baby mama." Once she gets knocked up, she goes to see the councilor and tells that person her baby daddy ran off. They then sign her up for food stamps, section 8 housing, a cell phone, WIC and every other welfare program offered by the government paid for with our tax money. As long as Cedrick is working, and only working 30 hours a week or less, no one comes after him for child support. Cedrick was also careful not to leave his clothes lying around the house in case a DFACS caseworker showed up and discovered him living in the government-provided apartment.

Cedrick also has a second vehicle, the one his baby mama normally drives. His tricked out Cadillac is never parked at the public housing complex so that the DFACS folks won't find out he actually makes well over $100,000 a year selling drugs. Cedrick has an income most of us would envy and not only does he make it tax free, but his living expenses are all taken care of by the taxpayers. His income is not $100,000; his disposable income is $100,000.

Cedrick knows what he is doing is wrong, but why stop? Going to prison doesn't scare him or getting a cap popped into his brain by a rival drug dealer does not scare him either. Yet this is a man that could awe you with his brilliance. He could be someone people would look up to, a real benefit to our society. But, no, he has learned to game the system and that is all right with him.

I do not know whatever became of Cedrick. After I moved on to another restaurant, I never saw him again. Cedrick did teach me though that our society's desire to help the poor has failed miserably. We are allowing generation after generation to scam the system just as Cedrick has his entire life. His mother also lived on welfare and, despite the reforms of the 1990's, Cedrick's children will likely follow the same path assuming they are not the victims of a drive-by shooting. Now, is it racist for me to tell this pitiful true story? No, because you will find people of all colors, shapes and sizes scamming the system.

Recently, I was at Wal-Mart. The woman in front of me in the checkout line was morbidly obese and she had waddled up to the cashier with a buggy filled to overflowing with potato chips, snack cakes and every other artery-clogging foodstuff imaginable. I watched as she pulled out a large package of t-bone steaks and wondered to myself if she could devour all those steaks in one sitting. I know; that was wrong of me. But I had seen those packages of steaks at the meat counter and even on sale they were too expensive for the Hudson family, so I really kind of envied her ability to afford that much high end food.

So you can imagine my fury when she whipped out an EBT card to pay for those steaks and other groceries. But it gets better – oh, so much better – that it became an interesting saga to watch unfold. There was not enough money on the buffarilla's government-issued card to pay for everything. She began putting items back and what did she put back? Not the Ho-Hos and certainly not the t-bones. No, she put back orange juice and the other items in the buggy that were actually healthy. The poor cashier had to stand there while this orang-utan crossed with a buffalo debated what to put back. It was about that time that a skinny man, probably in his mid 50s, showed up at her side. He was holding a case of Coors Light. Once she finished with her EBT order, she whipped out a $20 bill and bought the man's beer.

I had to clamp my lips shut.

The buffarilla in question was just as white as I am, so don't tell me criticizing welfare recipients is racist. This wasn't some poor soul still traumatized over the slavery that kept her family under the thumb of the Man. This was not someone who through past oppression thought she somehow had a special right to government largess. Indeed she was not someone who could claim Jim Crow had ruined her destiny or that of her grandparents before her. But before I judge, as the Bible tells us not to do, she or the man she was with might have some health condition that qualified them for EBT. But is it too much to ask that if we, the taxpayers, are going to put the food on her table that she consume food that is not going to make her fatter? If they have a medical condition that requires taxpayers' assistance, is it too much for us to ask that they lay off the beer and chips? I have someone who makes those demands on me every day: my kid. If I don't take care of her with all my resources, I will lose her and I know it. That fact means I keep myself and my lifestyle in line.

There can be no better illustration than Peggy Joseph who is commonly and fondly remembered as Peggy the Moocher. If you remember it was Peggy who found herself a television star after she blurted out on camera that she no longer had to worry about putting gas in her car or paying her mortgage thanks to President Barak Obama. It is undeniable that free school lunch, free rent, free health care, free child care and free food are powerful motivators to show up and cast a ballot. And who could forget the woman who recently was recently filmed screaming about her free "Obama phone?" To further point out that both political parties are complicit in swelling the welfare rolls to grab votes, it was the Reagan administration that began giving out free telephones and the George W. Bush administration that expanded the program and added cell phones to the original land line offer. Yep, Republicans pander to the poor just like our Democrat friends.

It is abundantly clear that our current class of elected leaders is not going to do anything about the massive theft that is our welfare system. Conservatives lack the desire to do anything because they are already beaten down with the race club. Liberals turn their heads because welfare recipients are the same ones that are packed into church buses and taken to the polls to vote for liberals who will keep the money flowing. It's payback for the t-bones.

True progressive thinkers admit there is a problem, but they claim in the hopes of saving people that we must expect some are going to play the system for what it is worth. It cannot be avoided, they say. My reaction is to say to you: get in your car and take a tour of your local public housing warehouse. What you will likely see in your city is what I see in mine and that is able bodied men shuffling along with their pants around their knees idle when most of us are out working for a living. You see able-bodied men sitting on the front porch with a cold 40-ounce beer at 10 a.m. when the rest of us are working. Rarely do you see grandma or a person in a wheelchair or someone who really deserves public help hanging out in front of the warehouses for the poor. What you see are the moochers during the daytime and those same folks become criminals at nightfall. I know this to be true, I am a reporter, and part of my beat is the crime beat.

What is terrible is that these are the same young men on some form of public assistance who tend to commit home invasions and armed robberies. So, the only conclusion is that taxpayers are bankrolling the ability of these people to commit crime. Sorry, the statistics on this do not lie. That red handkerchief hanging out of that droopy back pocket is indicative of the gang the individual belongs to and you and I are providing the means for this sick lifestyle by paying for their shelter, food and healthcare.

We, the people who have those little deductions on our paychecks, are bankrolling this segment of our society and it is long past time for us to say enough! The politicians who pander to that segment should be shamed out of office. While I really admired Cedrick for his mental acuity, I despised his lifestyle. Cedrick needed to work for what he got and commit to work that is legal and pay taxes like I do and I said so to him. But thanks to the War on Drugs and the current welfare system, he will keep on down his path until destruction of some kind of bad end finally catches up with him. If Cedrick wants to live the life of a gangsta, fine. I just believe that I should not have to pay to subsidize his lifestyle. In fact, while the War On Drugs itself has been a dismal failure, regular drug testing for welfare recipients would help to curb the abuse. Cedrick told me that he never actually used the stuff he sold so a test would not snag him, but drug testing would take away quite a number of his clientele.

The same goes for the buffarilla in the grocery store when we discuss controlling how our tax funded welfare money is spent. An EBT card should be used for celery, carrots, potatoes, and other staples. When Cheetos and sodas are scanned, the card should be programmed not to pay for it. These warehouses we call public housing complexes should be gated with key card access to only the people who really need to live there. Welfare counselors should advise young men like Cedrick that if they have children to GET A REAL JOB. Yes,

I know digging ditches and picking fruit in the orchards is hard work, but the illegal aliens from Mexico do not seem to mind it. After the grafters fall off the system, what would be left are the ones truly in need of assistance.

If the benefits were taken away, the ones that are gaming the system would either be forced to get a job, or they would die of starvation and I am fine with either of those outcomes. We, as a society can just simply take the children away into foster care if the adults agree to starvation for themselves. Don't tell me there is not a job to be found, I have never had much trouble finding one no matter how much I might not have liked the work.

My father died of cancer when I was 12 years old. We were not a rich family at the time of Dad's death. He was the service director of a car dealership and a part time minister, so we had stuff, but not anything above normal middle class. Dad's cancer treatment cost the family; his burial expenses cost the family as well. My mother had always worked the job she had loved and that was being a mommy. But at the age of 35, she found herself widowed with three small children on a limited income and she did what all responsible adults do: she got a job that paid more than hugs and kisses.

At age 13, I got a job as well. After begging and pleading with the guidance councilor at school, I secured a work permit even though I was two years too young to have one. I then went to a used car dealership and washed cars for minimum wage. A local camper dealer offered me more money, so I switched to washing and detailing travel trailers. The money I made did not support the family, but it meant we could all have pizza on Friday nights and Christmas was just as lavish for the younger ones as it always had been. Over the years, I worked in fast food, in a ceramics factory, an art shop and at the ripe old age of 17 managed a pizza delivery service. By the age of 18, I had hammered on the local radio programmers until one finally relented and gave me a board operator position.

Never once did the Hudson family even attempt to go on welfare, such a thing would have horrified my late father. We were determined to make it on our own. My mother sold my Dad's little fishing boat and I cried crocodile tears when I watched it wheeled away, but we survived and we survived without the help of the taxpayers. Had things been worse, my mother might have been forced to accept public assistance. She would have if that had been necessary, but I can guarantee we would not have been on the dole for long.

Why then does anyone tolerate the class who feels entitled to the contents of the American treasury? Again, what it is amounts to representation without taxation, which means naturally the people who are not paying the taxes but accepting the public dole as a career are only going to vote for people who allow it to continue. Both sides of that equation know the gig and are all comfortable keeping things the way that they are.

But I am not.

Getting rid of the politicians that support this behavior is not enough. It is now time for us to consider who among us should have the privilege to vote. As many have pointed out, there is no provision in the original Constitution that specifically determines voting to be a right. The franchise was originally deemed a privilege, that is, until some very well meaning people changed the Constitution and made it a right. Originally, it was landowners who could vote and that included women and free black folks, now it is anyone over the age of 18 years. That is a product of the democratization of America, but it is not a democratic principle. Those principles espoused by the Framers of this nation take into account that if everyone is allowed to vote the end result will be the chaos we are all now suffering.

Any politician who comes out publicly and says that to get a voter registration card, you should have to bring a tax return and prove that someone in your household pays taxes is going to get my vote. Even if the tax bill is only one dollar, voters should have to prove they pay taxes.

If this nation ever goes to a "fair tax" or consumption tax of some kind, then welfare recipients' names should be flagged in a database when they apply for the registration card. Is that discrimination? Yes. Does it bother me? Not in the least. If I were ever forced on welfare, I would happily give up the privilege to vote. That fact alone would keep me off of welfare. Besides, people who are on welfare should be out looking for work and not whittling away their time waiting in line for an open voting booth.

Again, the language in the amendment should be simple; anyone under the legal retirement age who does not have a debilitating medical condition should prove they pay some form of tax to vote. College students, the elderly, members of the military and spouses of taxpayers can be exempt. It could be property tax, taxes on investments, federal or state income tax, something, just prove you are a taxpayer. What about those who pay taxes, but get them all back at the end of the year? Well, they paid the tax, so let them vote.

What about people who honestly cannot find a job? Sorry, sit out this election cycle and worry about providing for your family, then come back when you have pulled yourself up by the bootstraps and are off the public dole. What about single mothers who can't help it that they are abandoned with children? My mother was abandoned due to a thing called death and our family never once left the tax rolls. My mother also voted at every opportunity.

The fourth plank of the Contract On The Government is to demand representation only for those who are actually paying the taxation unless there is a compelling reason the said individual is exempt from taxes. While Americans are compassionate people, welfare needs to be reigned in and given only to specific people who can prove need for a specific and limited period of time. Each person receiving welfare should be randomly drug tested and forced to submit to job training or education of some kind. As a prerequisite for obtaining welfare, the recipient should also agree to commit to 8 hours of community service per month. They should be required to give back to the community that is giving to them.

Naturally, most progressives are going to have a problem with taking away the franchise from anyone. They will cry racism and elitism and point out the 18th Amendment would have to be repealed to do such a thing. There is also the bureaucracy that would be created to process the paperwork needed allow a voter, any voter, to cast a ballot. So, it may be that while trying to ensure the rights of the taxpayers may sound great, it likely will face tough opposition from the people who think America is a democracy. However, if the other language of this plank is at the least enacted, the nation will spend less money and eliminate a large portion of people voting only for politicians who will continue and extend their ill-gotten benefits.

No matter how it is done, domestic welfare in America simply must be curtailed. It is important to note that we have always had a form of "welfare" in this country and it historically has been a system administered by churches. In a congregation, everyone tithes 10%, so naturally the wealthier pay more and the less fortunate pay less. The penniless are the recipients as the church uses the extra funds to help the less fortunate. That is why churches set up food banks and temporary shelters. At this point, though, we are taxing the wealthy to a degree that they cannot tithe as much as they normally would and giving the money away to people who, in the third world would be considered as wealthy.

It should also be noted that there is a very big difference between an entitlement and welfare. An entitlement is something that is earned, whereas welfare is legal theft.

The fourth plank of the Contract On The Government would also likely save lives since gang bangers would have less time available to gang bang. People like Cedrick might also live up to their potential and become people we can look up to rather than pity or despise. Most importantly, without sincere welfare reform what is left of the middle class will continue to be taxed out of existence while the welfare rolls and the recipients grow fatter. If we, as a people, remove the ability for representation without taxation to exist then we have taken a major step in defeating tyranny.

The city I live in is identical to most medium sized cities across the nation. There is an urban core followed by a ring of suburbs that is set up sort of like Dante's hell, the richer people tend to live in the outer rings. As you move past the 'burbs, you begin to see pine trees and fields with grazing cattle. The entire area is carved up into districts and you would assume that it is the furthest rings away from the urban core that receive the majority of farm subsidies. In that, you would assume wrong.

According to the Department of Agriculture, the district in Augusta receiving the most subsidies is district 1, the urban core. It makes one wonder if these people are keeping chickens in their loft apartments and growing cornfields on the top of high rise buildings. District 1 also has the highest concentration of public housing and Section 8 tenants. So, the fine residents of district 1 get free housing, free food, free medical care, multiple free cell phones and farm subsidies. When they get old, they can collect Social Security on wages they never earned. God forbid they chip a nail getting onto the public transportation bus because then they would fucking qualify for disability!

It is also worth noting that district 1 also boasts having the highest crime rate out of all of the 10 districts. The good folks in our city have learned that it is not wise to attempt a moonlight stroll along Riverwalk Park on the Savannah because you are more likely to have your ass beaten with a baseball bat and mugged than you are of in danger of slipping and falling into the river.

Chapter 5.
Paying To Be Disrespected Abroad

While it should be abhorrent to the working class that they must budget for Ramen Noodles while others swipe a card for free t-bones, The United States has another form of welfare that is also emptying the treasury. What I am saying? The treasury is already empty, that last sentence should have read - driving the country deeper into debt needlessly. That other sucking sound of welfare I would like for you to listen out for is in the form of foreign assistance. Some of that assistance is being given to countries that are hostile to America and her democratic principles.

During World War II, America bombed, shot and torpedoed Germany and Japan into submission. Had the Allies simply walked away like they did in 1918, the innocent people in those countries would have starved, rioted and possibly fallen back into nationalism, fascism and militarism. America and her allies chose wisely and aided the former Axis countries in rebuilding. Certainly that ambitious rebuilding came along with a huge financial cost to the victors, but it was one that was repaid. Such a thing came with great risk and there was no guarantee that the conquered nations wouldn't take the financial help and then elect another leader the likes of Hitler. But the foreign aid programs were a success, Germany and Japan became economic powerhouses and the trade between those nations and ours became mutually beneficial.

All you have to do is think Volkswagen and Sony mixed with McDonalds and Microsoft and you can conjure the lovely vision of our fat asses squeezing out of a compact car and waddling into the house with a bag of McLarders to spend the evening propped up in front of the television watching Netflix. That was a joke. You can laugh. Well, maybe.

The Berlin Airlift taught Americans that people abroad are deserving of humanitarian aid if they come around to believe in the principles of liberty. There is no freer nation hardly in the world today than Germany; you just can't parade around in Nazi attire, which seems a fine rule with most people. Across the world from Hitler's former stomping grounds, Japan has become the little nation that could. They are pumping out cars and electronics, building skyscrapers, and introducing a generation of Americans to sushi, sake and something called Anime porn faster than most people can text LOL.

Those examples are the successes, but there have been some serious and prolonged blunders. While many Americans are losing homes, growing gardens to avoid the grocery store and skimping on the offering plate out of necessity, the national government is garnishing wages in the form of taxes and sending the money to warlords overseas.

The legislatively created United States Agency for International Development, or USAID, likes to boast that the foreign aid money they spend is less than one half of one percent of the federal budget. That assertion, upon inspection, is misleading. That percentage is based on what they spend on assistance and not what it costs them to spend what they spend. Federal agencies love to twist statistics and in the interest of transparency baffle the reader with silly charts that are as vague as road signs that say "slow children at play." Is it, slow-children at play, slow children - at play, or slow-children at-play? You get the point.

If you read the full text and do not rely only on the charts of USAID's 2009 annual report then you will learn that the budget expenses for the group was over $11 billion during that fiscal year, not $11 million as the graphs seem to indicate. According to their own statistics, USAID only spent 13% of their budget on humanitarian assistance. A larger number, 28% was spent on something called "investing in people" and another 16% was spent on "governing justly and democratically."

The administration (salaries) cost the agency over $144 million in the 2009 fiscal year. After all of the non-aid money is rolled into the total amount spent on foreign aid, it is easy to see that more than a just a tiny fraction of the federal budget is spent each year. The worst part is America is currently borrowing money to send it overseas.

The next step in following the money and becoming infuriated is to look at some of the countries on the receiving end. It just so turns out that the country of Sudan is tops on our list. Groups such as Amnesty International and celebrity music performers have made much of the situation in the African continental horn country of Sudan. The situation really is bad on the ground in that country.

In the Darfur region of Sudan, genocide has occurred there for many years and continues to this day. A government-backed militia known as the Janjaweed has done far more than just terrorize the population. They kill, they rape, they maim and they torture. People willing to risk their lives to go into the region and gain information have duly documented all of this. Celebrity warbler Yoko Ono allowed her late husband's music to be recorded and sold royalty free by a group of musicians who wanted to do the right thing and raise money for the refugees. Those actions are worthy of praise.

What is not worthy of praise is that, according to their own documents, USAID has spent $6 billion dollars on aid to Sudan in the years between 2004 and 2009. What that has amounted to is not Volkswagens and Sonys emanating out of that country. It has been the exact opposite. The government in charge has accepted the money and continued about its murderous ways. They know the diplomats in the United States will save face in the world and shrug their shoulders hoping next year's installment of funds will cause some spark of change in their hearts, but America would never commit to military action to reclaim the misspent funds. They know that because they learned from a neighbor country, one called Somalia. Most Americans know Somalia from the motion picture Black Hawk Down. The saga happened when good-hearted America decided to undertake an unprecedented humanitarian military exercise and bring food to the starving people. For years, Somalia, like many other countries in the region had endured a tribal civil war. The mission of the American troops was to secure the ground for the arrival and disbursal of the supplies. One major obstacle of the mission was a warlord by the name of Mohamed Farrah Aidid. The US military tried to secure the capital of Mogadishu for the aid arriving on the ground by rounding up this ruffian. Not only was the mission a disaster, with the military outnumbered by armed clansmen, but also the Somali "citizens" repaid America's kindness by dragging the bodies of dead marines through the streets of the capital.

So, the State Department learned its lesson, right? Why give out food and medical supplies when the people in power are just going to kill the soldiers bringing the aid and steal the supplies for themselves, right? America wouldn't just cower to the humiliation and continue to give aid money that came from the table of taxpayers, right?

Wrong.

In fiscal year 2010, more than $31 million dollars was given to the Somalian government. The years 2009 and 2010 were also the years the world watched over and again as Somali pirates routinely hijacked and ransomed off cargo ships from around the world in defiance of the United States and its millions of dollars in aid money. It is crazy that the US government ignores the folks struggling financially in America while giving billions of dollars away to rogue and violent anarchy-ridden countries abroad.

The whole idea of USAID, not to be too redundant, is to aid developing countries. Well, perhaps common sense might one day dictate the national government should only attempt to develop countries that are worthy of and can actually be developed. If the information presented here has not made you mad enough, consider this: according to USAID, there are 3.2 million people in Somalia in need of emergency assistance. In the 2010 fiscal year, the national government spent $31 million dollars in aid to Somalia. Just so that we are all operating on or over an 8th grade educational level, will you pull out the calculator and divide 31 by 3.2, please? My math averages that out to about $100,000 for every man, woman, and child in emergency need this year in Somalia, and those people killed American soldiers and continue pester merchant mariners!

It gets worse.

In 2000, the year before America was brutally attacked by former "freedom fighters" supported by the CIA, the country of Afghanistan was given 54 million dollars in aid. That number swelled in 2007 to over 5 billion, according to data from the U.S. Census Bureau, and that is because America now has to rebuild the country that virtually attacked her. Before September 11, 2001, aid money was flowing like candy into the very camps that were training people to fly planes into the Pentagon and World Trade Towers. In modern lingo, we paid to be disrespected. The very people we were subsidizing bloodily disrespected our country.

Am I the only one who thinks this is pure lunacy?

Well-meaning people sometimes do stupid things. One of my friends (and believe it or not, he is a local elected official) has several rental properties in a nice middle class suburb here in Augusta. He allowed a fellow to move in to one of his houses without signing a real lease or submitting to a background check. Months into the lease, the tenant who we will call the "fellow" missed the rent and electricity payment. He had a good excuse, or so it seemed to the friend-of-mine-who-happens-to-be-an-elected-official who we will call "Gas Cap."

Gas Cap inquired of the fellow on the matter of the months long overdue bills that were piling up and the fellow always had a good excuse. The fellow would come back with things like

"My truck broke down,"

"It rained so much this month that I hardly worked,"

"My girlfriend is in rehab,"

"Argentina's GDP just dropped by 2 percentage full points and I lost my ass in day trading!"

Gas Cap bought every excuse from the fellow even while he noticed the economy was tanking on him and he really needed that fellow's rent money. Unfortunately, things began to go south quickly financially and Gas Cap had to start using his credit card to pay for what he needed, including the mortgage payments on the property that was occupied by the fellow and his rehab girlfriend. On one occasion Gas Cap was called to the house because the air conditioner was broken and he immediately noticed that the fellow had adopted several cats. The house reeked with the smell of cat piss. The stench was so bad that Gas Cap could hardly breathe while he was checking out the air unit.

Months went by and my friend kept paying the mortgage, electricity, water, insurance and tax bills on the property when the fellow still refused to pay rent or even attempt to catch up on past bills. Gas Cap got to the point where he had to cut off cable television service to his own house because his budget was under such strain. The fellow in his rental house had not only backed out on a year's worth of rent, but his cats had damaged the carpets and walls throughout the house and he had let the once manicured gardens in the front yard go to seed. Since the fellow refused to water the garden, the plants all dried out and died. Adding to the insult and injury, the fellow had dumped a messy pile of junk in the rear grounds of the property.

Gas Cap finally got mad.

He told the fellow he had 30 days to get out or the fellow would have to dodge the bulldozer he was sending out to the property. Well, I embellish. The real way it went down was Gas Cap finally wised up and told the guy to get out or he was cutting off the electricity and the water. Gas Cap finally realized that his good-hearted spirit had been taken for a ride that someone else enjoyed and that he had paid for it all. The fellow moved out and moved on to his next potential victim.

The only difference between Gas Cap and the federal government of the United States is that not only has the US paid with a credit card for a neighbor to live rent free; the US supported the neighbor knowing that the neighbor was beating his wife and raping his own daughter while letting the cats piss on the walls. Unlike Gas Cap, the federal government has not wised up and cut off the funding, rather it has ramped up assistance for countries that are totally undeserving. America's ambassadors cut checks to these countries and have been slaughtered for their efforts…Yes, I am talking about Benghazi, Libya.

Former Soviet satellite states have come around to embracing liberty. One of those countries is Turkmenistan and it sits just to the northern border of our Iranian friends. The country is a constitutional republic governing a people that are mostly Muslim. A holdover from the Soviet era is that the executive branch of the country holds most of the power and tends to be authoritarian. However, Turkmenistan is a relatively peaceful country internally despite facing 60% unemployment and so far this little republic has attacked none of her neighbors.

Turkmenistan is largely irrigated desert, and what do you generally find under desert sand? Yes, that would be oil. The Turkmenistanians are sitting on vast deposits of oil and natural gas; the problem is that they have no way to export their treasure. Maybe I am crazy and you should use this very nicely articulated piece of trash book you wasted money on as a doorstop, but wouldn't it make more sense to send Turkmenistan $6 billion to help put those people to work retrieving their oil rather than give it to Sudanese warlords, Egyptian Islamists and other governments that are sworn to the destruction of Western culture?

According to the very same U.S. Census data, while in 2007 we gave Cambodia $71 million, $184 million to Mexico, and $53 million to Morocco, but we gave Turkmenistan virtually nothing.

The ones who favor giving money to the American soldier murdering, rioting in the streets, pirating of ships Somalis will say if U.S. foreign aid were withdrawn the country would break down into lawless chaos. The country is already in chaos and has been for years, what our money is doing is funding the chaos. In this case, just like with old Gas Cap, we are being nothing more than enablers.

As a people, we must wrap our brains around the fact that not every society in the world is ready for the democratic principles espoused by America. Our history shows that we had to fight 3 wars on this continent before the concept of liberty was institutionalized. The French, who we love to malign, also had to go through a hideous civil war starring the guillotine before individual liberty became a cherished concept in that nation. While we should feel sorry for the Sudanese who are being slaughtered in Darfur, we have to understand that America cannot end all of the world's suffering.

When a people are ready for the concept of liberty, they will do what Crispus Attucks did in 1770 and stand up to tyranny (look him up; it's a great story). When it becomes a common understanding among a society that all are created equal and have the God given right to a pursuit of happiness, they will do what Washington, Jefferson, Adams and the other framers of our republic did: fight to win liberty or die trying.

It would be the hope of humankind that the people of Sudan, Congo and Somalia could one day enjoy the liberty enjoyed by the people of Raleigh, North Carolina. However, the good people of Raleigh cannot buy liberty for the folks in Darfur. It can only happen when the people of Darfur get tired of being shown on television commercials starring Sally Struthers, having horse-riding terrorists invading their fields and living under an oppressive regime that rapes and maims them leaving them to starve in the streets. Those people have to get tired of tyranny and they themselves have to rise up against the tyranny. We cannot do it for them and we certainly should not be whipping out the national credit card over the matter, but that is exactly what we are doing.

Following this line of thinking, the same should be applied to states that have declared themselves enemies of the United States. Now, there are the scare-d-cats that will remind that if we yank aid away from North Korea, they will go nuclear. Here is a hint: They are already nuclear. Yank the funding, yank the armistice, declare war on those people and tell the Russians and Chinese to sit down and shut up and finish the damn thing like it should have been finished in 1950. Enough said.

Plank five of the Contract On The Government is to curtail spending on non-essential foreign aid. This does not require an amendment or a bill before Congress. All this plank requires is a little common sense. If a developing country accepts aid from this nation, then there must be some reciprocity. It is the receiving country's responsibility to develop and join the global trading family if they accept our largess. Otherwise, just like the able bodied American that refuses to be responsible, we should leave the people in those countries to their own fate.

Chapter 6.
Permanent Binding Alliances

George Washington understood that politics and national policy are fluid concepts. Today you may be friends with X and against what Z is attempting to do to X. Yet, tomorrow, it may be X treating Z badly and you find your alliances have changed. France came to the aid of the colonies battling the British during the Revolution. However, years later when France went to war with Britain, President Washington politely declined to involve the United States. He basically said the conflict was none of our business and signed a neutrality proclamation.

In his farewell address, Washington warned against permanent alliances and Thomas Jefferson went on later to parrot Washington's words. In today's world, America is involved in many complicated, permanent and expensive alliances that need to be re-thought. Few lay people anywhere can point out what the United Nations has done that is beneficial to world security other than spend Ted Turner's money for him. To a degree, that has kept America safe from Ted Turner. The UN is to be lauded for its programs to combat world hunger and AIDS. But otherwise, it has been an organization that has allowed the very opponents of liberty gain an international voice and audience.

Congress very rightly stomped on President Wilson's dream, the

League of Nations, the UN's precursor. They understood the idea of a League was a global "democracy" with tyrannical nations having the same standing as nations based upon liberty. Despite all the League's attempts at appeasement and renditions of "Kumbaya," we still got World War II. Rather than a glorious League that would build upon liberty and spread it to the corners of the globe, the globe became infested with Communism, Fascism and National Socialism. The League may have combated Malaria and Cholera, but it also fostered the spread of Rabies.

The modern UN is nothing more than a super-sized version of the old League. It has had no power to stop any of the modern genocides that have occurred. The UN has not acted against the abusive and genocidal mandates of Sharia law, which is in some form in place in every country in the world that has the word "Islamic" before the word "republic." The UN has failed to bring any semblance of peace to the Middle East or to the Koreas and has stood back impotently in Sudan. Even worse, countries that routinely ignore what are considered the basic tenets of human rights sit on the panels and committees that discuss and implement the UN's human rights policies. What is sad is that all of that is old news.

The Senate refused to enroll the United States into the League of Nations because they knew the Versailles Treaty was a piece of shit and it was eventually going to lead to another world war. In the modern world, we know for a fact the UN wants sovereignty for itself, yet is as effective as the League was in dealing with conflict among its' members. The UN will eventually allow for if not cause another world war and history backs up that assertion.

The problems with the United Nations have been documented time and again. Long before the September 11th, 2001 attacks, the UN was very much aware that the women of Afghanistan were treated worse than the camels in that nation and they did nothing. The UN was aware of the butchering in the Congo and they did nothing. The UN was around for Cambodia and raised nary a word when Saddam Hussein went on his murderous gassing sprees in Iraq. It has become a regular event to see thugs such as Hugo Chavez, Mahmoud Ahmadinejad and Fidel Castro using the vaunted podium at the UN to spew their absurd ranting. Two of these men are almost literally the progeny of Adolf Hitler. Ahmadinejad regularly denies what America documented conclusively as a Jewish Holocaust and the late Chavez's country is exactly the spot where many of the beaten Nazi's fled to and hid out after the war. In today's world, knowing what happened in 1939, would we negotiate with Hitler? I think not.

A world body today is unnecessary overkill, just as were the domestic overreaches of Teddy Roosevelt and Woodrow Wilson, et al. The UN is another bloated worthless bureaucracy that stands in the way of progress every time it attempts to act in a progressive manner. How is it that the sovereign United States needs to go before the United Nations and ask permission to expel Saddam Hussein's Iraq from his neighbor, a US ally, Kuwait? How is it that when we receive that "resolution," that the UN then dictates the terms of our military endeavor?

Sure, the Persian Gulf conflict was a coalition of forces from many nations. But if the United States decides to commit herself to an act of war, the Constitutional method must be applied. After that, the sovereign United States can tell the rest of the world to either join the bandwagon of liberty or fuck off. America should not allow the UN or anyone else to tell the generals of the army of this country how they may fight a war if what they are doing is within the bounds of the Geneva Convention. We used to have this concept called "unconditional surrender" and thanks to the UN we have moved to surrender-if-it-meets-with-approval-of-the-Security-Council-demands-on-how-America-exercises-its-sovereignty.

There are diplomats in this country that know how to argue on this nation's behalf directly to other nations as set forth in the US Constitution. We do not need the approval and consent of Russia and China to manage our interests. If the Swiss decide they will not extradite an admitted pedophile to face justice, well then fine. Our diplomat should go to Switzerland and say 'fine, you can keep Roman Polanski on your soil and while you are at it, why don't you finally come clean on your nation's complicity in financing the Nazis?' And if some computerized leak website posts such language back and forth from this country to another, then so-the-hell-be-it. We will just act like a sovereign nation and find a better way to protect our official communications.

It is almost bizarre beyond comprehension that the very type of people my grandfather fought and was wounded in his quest to annihilate before they annihilate him, are now allowed to come to New York City, stay in luxury accommodations, eat the finest American foods, take a dump on a nice porcelain toilet and then strut onto a worldwide stage and criticize the very country that is their host. I do not think we should be forced to allow their waste in our sewer system.

Because of the continued hand wringing at the UN, the Korean Conflict has managed to span over a half of a century. Over there, the situation on the ground is simple. One half of Korea enjoys building Hyundais and forcing Kim Chi on the rest of the world and the other half worships a dictator as a god and is trying to force the worship of the Dear Leader on the rest of Korea. Rather than simply deal with the problem, get it over with and bring our kids in the service home, America cannot so much as belch at the DMZ on the 38th parallel without the expressed consent of the United Nations. Naturally, what is the policy to deal with a rogue, militarized regime that is sinking a peaceful nation's ships, bombarding their territory and waving nuclear weapons in the face of everyone in the world? Why, let's give them money!

Due to the treaties that we have with the Republic of Korea, America is morally and legally bound to protect this important friend nation and trading partner. This is not an all encompassing permanent bond, but an agreement between two nations that trade heavily with one another. The Russians should have no say in our foreign policy on this matter and neither should China. If those countries are tired of refugees from North Korea and having to feed the masses there, then those countries should tell North Korea to get with the rest of the world's program and stop threatening their peaceful neighbor. It is as simple as that, and that simple idea came not from a group of diplomats, but from an ordinary American citizen, me.

Like other rogue nations, America should not be sending money or grain to North Korea if they continue to buy bullets instead of food for their people and use their bullets to threaten their neighbor. We should let them starve. If Russia wants to give them food, then fine, but Plank number five of the Contract should apply to Kim Jong Un and his minions. If the UN has a problem with America withdrawing aid from that militaristic and nutty regime, then it is their problem to stew over. There is no such thing as sovereignty for a "world body."

Over time, the national government has ceded quite a bit of America's sovereignty in foreign affairs to the UN and that is absolutely unconstitutional. The world should have input but no decision making power on the sovereignty of the United States. A United Nations without the United States is the only possibility for America to regain her sovereignty against the forces that are committed to doing her harm.

The sixth plank of the Contract On The Government is that this nation immediately severs all ties and rejects all responsibilities to the United Nations. The national government of the United States does not have the Constitutional authority to cede sovereignty to any power other than the people of this country as per the 10th Amendment. If the UN chooses to keep its headquarters in New York, as long as they are paying property taxes, then let them stay. However, if the UN decides to host a foreign leader of a country that is at war with the United States, then the national government will reserve the right to arrest that person as a person at war-declared with this country.

You might ask, well, there are some countries that want to arrest certain members of our national government. What do we do if Switzerland arrests Henry Kissinger or any other American they believe has acted against the dictates of the so-called World Court? The simple answer is that Mr. Kissinger nor any other American citizen should travel to a country that does not have a direct treaty relationship with the US that recognizes our judicial system as having sovereignty over citizens of this country providing the individual did not commit a specific crime on that specific country's soil. Sorry Henry, we cannot help you if you go to France and pee on the Mona Lisa. However, France should not be able to arrest a citizen of this country based on the whim of the "international community." Should they do so, it should be considered an act of war.

One of my favorite treaties of all time is the Progressive era Kellogg-Briand Pact. This document was sponsored by the League of Nations and signed by the US, France, Britain, Germany, Italy and Japan in 1928. What Kellogg-Briand did was outlaw aggressive war. I am not being facetious when I say it is a favorite. Of course, a decade later, all the parties that signed the treaty would be locked in the grips of what became World War II, but the idea was novel. It was also naive. You cannot outlaw conflict, it will never happen. But the idea that learned men did once try is, I don't know, worth putting a smile on your face. Just like Kellogg-Briand, the UN is a naive concept and one that would have caused George Washington to shudder.

A quick search engine query using the terms "U.N. + condemns" will yield over 1,920,000 results. Over time, the UN has condemned everything from North Korean nuclear tests to Malaria. Despite the condemnations, the North Koreans are still building bombs and sinking ships and mosquitoes continue to defy the world body by biting people and spreading disease. In fact, the UN could go so far as to condemn itself and it is likely nothing would happen.

In this century, America is dealing with war in Afghanistan and Iraq. This country is at a "shooting-stalemate" with North Korea. All of the borders of the country of Iran are either American possessions by default, or are allies with the US meaning future conflict is almost assured. Despite years of negotiation trying to move towards peace in the Middle East, success has eluded the people there to this point. The "Arab Spring" has become the Sharia Law Takeover.

An America that is giving its foreign aid to developing trading partners and not hostile forces can handle the world stage by herself. She never did and does not now need the United Nations. If they want us to continue sending a representative, then fine, we can. I suggest we send the thousands of illegal Mexicans invading our southern states. The UN better have lots of beer on hand as every Mexican I have ever met can drink me far under the table.

Anyone arguing that plank six is an isolationist rant is absolutely wrong. America's greatest triumphs have not been in war, but in spreading our concepts and innovations across the globe. Karl Benz of Germany invented the automobile, but it was Henry Ford of the United States that brought it to the world. It was the Wright brothers of the United States that brought powered human flight to the world. Computers would likely still be the size of a desk without the work of American Bill Gates and his contemporaries. There was no country in the world that practiced the democratic ideals based upon liberty until a group of Americans defined the concept, and they did so through the US Constitution. This country did not spread innovation through the act of committee, but rather through individual leadership.

This nation does not have to withdraw from global affairs. Indeed, just the opposite is true. America has long been the leader of progress on the world stage. We can trade with any nation that wants to trade with us and we can partner with nations so they may practice liberty and avoid outside aggression. Alliances are a necessary thing, but permanent alliances are the recipe for disaster.

George Washington understood that no alliance is really permanent. Just as personal friendships are fluid, so too are the friendships of nations. Naturally, men have come to the enlightened viewpoint that compromise by words is far more palatable than resolution through armed force. Yet, conflict is a part of the human experience. Conflict is almost always resolved quicker and to better satisfaction when worked out between the parties involved rather than by the decree of a third party.

The United States cannot withdraw within her own borders and ignore the rest of the world. But if we toe the line of being Washingtonian Constitutionalists, then we will lead by example and expect the rest of the world to stand with us. There is no reason to abandon NATO or tell the Canadians we will no longer sign treaties on trade and mutual defense. What Washingtonian Constitutionalism is all about is respecting that the sovereignty of the United States rests in the hands of the citizens of the country and wielded through the nation's founding document. Therefore, there is no need for a global authority since the Constitution does not specifically call for the adherence to one.

Under strict definition, it is not legal for the United States to belong to the United Nations if membership means this country must cede portions of its sovereignty. The sixth plank of the Contract On The Government is the demand for immediate and total withdrawal from the United Nations.

Chapter 7.
The Hideous Pig of the Federal Bureaucracy

It has become a fun pastime of mine to count how many "conservative" politicians who stump on the concept of cutting spending and then get elected only to spend like the hooker on Rodeo Drive as portrayed by the lovely Julia Roberts in Pretty Woman. I think the operative word used in that flick was to spend an "obscene" amount of money and to trade in the slutty clothing in favor for Rodeo Drive couture. That is what Washington D.C. does every day, the Congress spends obscene amounts of money to create a facade. Only, once the politicians put nice clothes on the nation's whore of a bureaucracy, she doesn't suddenly gain manners and learn how to be ladylike at a polo match. No, our well-dressed hooker keeps on screwing people every opportunity she gets, even if it is on the field in plain view to everyone during our genteel polo game.

Over and over I hear so-called conservatives feed their willing sheeple the line they are going to cut taxes and cut spending. Yet, have you noticed that the cut taxes part is specific, "we are going to cut taxes for the middle class," but the cut spending side never really gets into what it is they want to cut? And why do politicians feel they must speak in the royal plural? We don't have royalty in the US, so why do they feel the need to talk like the Queen. It is not "we are going to Washington to cut taxes," it is "I will…" That just bugs me, but we digress…again.

The conservatives never say specifically what they will cut from the budget. When an honest member of the media attempts to draw them out on this issue, they offer vague answers at best. "The federal bureaucracy is larger than it has ever been in the history of our union," they offer. Okay, tell us something we do not know! Where are you going to cut? If you are going to shrink the size of the government, then you are going to cut off some kind of service people have come to depend on and expect, so what is it?

I don't know is what they are really saying. Yet, throughout this book, I have identified key ways to restore the federal treasury. Doing so simply takes the will of the people of this country and the unified demand that politicians follow through with true reform. If states and municipalities can find ways to streamline services and avoid operating in a deficit, then there is no reason the federal government cannot do the same. Yet, it hasn't saved one single penny in over a century. Politicians from both parties get red in the face when I encounter their vague platitudes about "shrinking government while investing in the future." Republicans and Democrats know both parties have allowed federal regulatory agencies to run so out of control with their red tape, restrictions and rules that companies that manufacture goods have run out of the country and set up sweat shops overseas. Both parties have allowed unions to influence regulation and legislation to the point that manufacturing companies were forced to relocate up to Canada or down to Mexico. Yeah, that has been a real good trade off; Mexico gets American jobs and we get their riff-raff illegally storming our borders. Speaking of the unions and the regulations, those companies that did stay and allowed themselves to edge on bankruptcy simply looked to the federal government for a bailout. In Chrysler's case, the government provided the money, but kept the union demands and the hideous pension system. In the end of that little story, the tax payers paid the bailout and allowed the failed system to operate. Did the union employees say thanks and get back to work? Nope, they continued business as usual and no one really said anything when Chrysler employees were caught sneaking off the job to a local park during their mandated 15 minute break and proceeded to get shit-faced drunk. Now those are exactly the people I want building the car my daughter rides in going to ballet on Thursdays.

The federal government has become so massive and overblown that no one person can rein it in. No one party will do it either. The political class will simply continue on with their party slogans until the next crisis occurs and then have some advertising executive come up with another meaningless tag line knowing the public will buy and go back to watching Wheel Of Fortune. However, if people elected at both the state and federal level work together they can find where the money drain is going and begin to plug the leaks. The challenge of finding exactly where to cut the fiscal fat can be met if the people force the politicians to lay their special interests aside and conduct the business vital to the nation. In the earlier chapters of this book, I have disclosed where billions and billions are going in domestic and foreign aid to people who do not deserve it and make it a lifestyle to demand more at either the point of a gun or an election. But the other giant sow that feeds from the trough of the people's money is the government bureaucracy itself. Following the planks of the Contract On The Government will, as Cicero once said, rebuild the treasury.

The formula for cutting the federal bureaucracy is simple and can be found explained succinctly in the 10th Amendment of the Constitution. Any child can understand the principle of "If I don't give you express permission to do something, then assume you can't do it." Here's how the framers put it on paper: The powers not delegated to the United States by the Constitution, nor prohibited by it to the States, are reserved to the States respectively, or to the people.

A simple rule of thumb is that any agency, department, bureaucracy or office or mandate that does not perform a function expressly given to the federal government should be abolished. The federal government may build roads, operate post offices, coin money and defend the nation. The government cannot, though, regulate the production or distribution of energy, public education, transportation within a state, lawful use of a firearm within a state or (my favorite) public housing.

One major leak in the hull of the federal government is within the Department of Housing and Urban Development. I briefly wrote earlier about the Laney Walker neighborhood district in my city of Augusta when discussing the abuse of earmarks; however the earmarks are pocket change when compared to the tax payer funds that are bled out by HUD. In Augusta, Laney Walker is a traditional African-American neighborhood, but I hate divisive hyphenated speak, so let's just say it is a traditionally black neighborhood. As a little boy, James Brown, the Godfather of Soul shined shoes on those streets. As a little girl, Butterfly McQueen walked those streets to school. Working with researcher Eric Montgomery with Historic Augusta, he and I found what appears to be her childhood home before she went on to fame in Gone With The Wind and later became a hero as a civil rights activist.

Laney Walker is the former home space of educator Lucy Craft Laney and has one of the earliest structures belonging to the African Methodist Episcopal Church within its borders. There is extraordinary history on almost every corner of the Laney neighborhood. Yet, it has remained a very poor neighborhood that was allowed to go to seed long before I was ever born. In 2000, our State Senator and majority leader in the state capitol, Charles Walker, created a non-profit group called the Augusta Neighborhood Improvement Corporation, or ANIC. During this same time, several faith-based Community Housing Development Organizations, or CHoDOs, sprang up. In other words, almost all of the CHoDOs operating here are a non-profit arm of a local church. The intent was that these groups would completely redevelop Laney Walker. ANIC was originally funded with $20 million from federal HUD, and they obtained other income streams from state sources as well.

Not only was ANIC funded by the federal government, but those earmarks on legislation also sent money to the CHoDOs. Exactly how much funding was hurled at the five square miles of Laney Walker will likely never be known. My figure puts it at nearly $70 million over a decade. The problem is that after all that funding, Laney Walker remains a demilitarized zone. No one really wants to live there because the people who do currently routinely kill each other.

Augusta is known internationally for the golf course on which the Masters Tournament is played each year. If you take a stroll on the tournament grounds, you can see that the Augusta National Golf Club spends some serious money on the course and surrounding areas each year. The result of that money spent can be seen all around; you can see it, touch it and smell it. The same cannot be said for Laney-Walker. The first thing I noticed that was odd was that ANIC did not seem to have any real plan on how to redevelop. Instead of bulldozing a city block and starting over, they cherry picked where they built houses. The result was a brand new, brick, three-bedroom single family home erected across the street from a tenement crack house.

The people at ANIC felt the Laney Walker district needed a "gated community," so they spent $600 thousand to build one. Only, after they were finished, there were only 4 small town home units built with no landscaping and no gate. The sign out front announced the starting price for the units at $139,000. This happened before America's troubles in the real estate market, so that wasn't the mark down price, it was the starting price. Follow me here; the figure 139 times 4 does not equal 600. ANIC built their "gated community with no gate" never even expecting to financially break even!

Two years later, ANIC got around to actually putting up the gate on The Enclaves, their gated pet project. They put it up after HUD gave them another $75,000 to build a fence and a gate that were already supposed to be there.

What happened to the man who conceived and funded ANIC? Mr. Charles Walker, the former Senator, is fulfilling the prison sentence of a federal jury. He was found guilty of fraud through his newspaper and charity organization. Walker went down in a 140 some odd felony count fireball. ANIC continues on and I have reported on how their tax returns are a laughable mess. They bought parking lots for obscene amounts of money and arrogantly started their own for-profit construction company using taxpayer dollars. Naturally, once I exposed the construction company, it was quietly folded. After my first round of questioning, ANIC unplugged its website and has left it unplugged for years. People wanting to buy a home through ANIC these days need to have ESP since the group does not advertise nor have a website. Sure, they are committed to putting people in new homes all right.

The problems are not only with ANIC, I have shown and proven how some of the churches sponsoring the CHoDOs have purchased land under the church's name and flipped the land over to their non-profit organization for a profit. HUD has deep pockets and they all know it and it has led to the taxpayers being exploited. It has taken a decade and millions of dollars of your money and my money to do almost nothing in the Laney Walker area except build a few houses that either no one wants to or can't afford to live in. These houses have their air conditioning units encased in steel wire mesh because people keep stealing the copper. That being known, who in their right mind would park a new car out in front of one of those houses every night?

The people at ANIC and the CHoDOs do not care that their mission is not being followed; they are getting their money and that is all that matters. They do not care if none of the houses they build sell because to them it is not about helping the less fortunate get a home of their own, but about getting money from the government to build a home or condo or a fence or whatever. Now, if we as a society pumped that kind of money into one tiny patch of land in Georgia, how much have we spent nationally?

The interesting thing is if you go to the folks at HUD on the national level and ask to track money that is believed to be missing, they will claim the money spent was not theirs to be stolen. Once an allocation is given to the recipient state on behalf of a group, the feds consider the money to be state money. Then you follow up and ask the state what happened to the money and they claim they gave it to the local municipality and so the money now belongs to them. If you question the municipality, they will tell you they were nothing more than a legal "conduit" for the group receiving the funding. At the end of a seemingly endless trail, the only conclusion that can be drawn is that the group applied for HUD funding, received HUD funding and even if they used the money for a drunken orgy in Las Vegas there is really no one to question them on it.

No one has questioned these groups except little bastards like me who refuse to let a dead dog lay and rot in the street. I have publicly taunted ANIC and the CHoDOs to prove me wrong. One of the men central to ANIC is a very powerful attorney here who acts as the attorney for two of our area's school boards. I have invited him to file a libel suit against me if any of my public assertions were wrong. We haven't received a peep from them. In this case, the FBI has told me to my face that they are not interested in pursuing the matter. If the FBI will admit severe irregularities but decline to investigate, then where is a citizen to go to report possible criminal activity?

I must state again that the message here is that if HUD blew a wad to the tune of multiple millions of dollars here in one tiny area of Augusta, how much has it peed away across the nation? I am willing to bet it is more than one interest payment on our deficit bill to China. There are plenty of federal agencies that act in the same arrogant manner when it comes to our tax dollars. They know there is no accountability and they do not care. Agencies such as HUD feel their job is simply to spend the money, but not to track where it eventually goes. Over time though, I have proven the money goes down a rabbit hole and into the pockets of people who have learned how to game the system. Occasionally, people like the esteemed former Georgia Senator Charles Walker get caught and sent to jail, but their minions remain and they continue to suck the money out of our wallets and place it in their own.

Not only is there not a provision in the U.S. Constitution stating that everyone has a right to affordable housing, the 10th Amendment clearly places such endeavors at the control of the several states. Why should the people of Houston, Texas pay for someone to have a home in Augusta, Georgia? If Texas has surplus funding and wants to use it to build houses, then the rest of the country should consider relocating to Texas where ranches are cheap and plentiful. However, demanding that the people of Texas contribute to an unconstitutional agency prone to giving away large sums of money to organizations that do nothing other than play fix-a-slum is something I would like to hear a politician speak out on when they preen about being the one to cut spending.

As the nation has seen with the recent housing crisis, the national government went even further than just granting a right to affordable housing. Out of nowhere, the right changed from that of access to affordable housing to a right to the funding for affordable housing. And, of course, it was the loan defaults made by recipients of Freddie Mae and Fanny Mac that lead to the rash of foreclosures. After living in a nice new house for several years and paying the equivalent of rent, people actually had an incentive to default and simply pay rent. When all of those new foreclosed houses suddenly landed on the market and banks were straddled with useless pieces of paper for loans, plenty of people who legitimately purchased their houses found themselves underwater due to property value decreases. Hence the domino effect that led to the latest recession and a real and possibly impending depression the likes to which this country has never experienced. What did HUD and ANIC and the CHoDOs do when the housing bubble burst? They built more houses and handed out more Fannie Mae applications, of course!

The point is that it is easy to find where to cut the federal budget. It is not hard for even the intellectually challenged to figure out that programs and services and rights not granted by the Constitution should not be endeavors of the federal government. Providing for the general welfare of the people means constructing roads and bridges that benefit everyone and not giving away houses and food and a free iPod to every person who finds him or herself living on American soil. The general welfare provision doesn't include building and selling houses any more than it does providing free internet porn for those who like to jerk off to dirty pictures.

Not only has the federal government stretched the Constitutions "provide for the general welfare" provision like taffy to claim people have a right to affordable housing, but there are other 'general welfare' boondoggles to be found. Under that provision, the government long ago concluded they have the right to tell people what they may drink or smoke in the privacy of their own homes. This right the government grabbed for itself worked so well for the Progressives in the early 20th Century that the idea for prohibition of alcohol turned to outlawing a weed that naturally grows from the ground. Every time the federal government feels the need to grow its power and interfere with the lives of citizens, they simply declare a war.

One of the biggest money bleeders in this nation's history is the War on Drugs. There are multiple agencies involved in this sham, including some in our intelligence community. How is it that we can use the might of American military power to force the Taliban from power in Afghanistan, but we are powerless to stop the average Afghan farmer from growing poppies? If poppies grow so well there then there must be some other more beneficial plant that could be planted and harvested. Not only is America seemingly unable to show the Afghans how to grow legal plants, the government cannot stop the rock stars, the Hollywood crowd and heiresses in California from using the Afghan's end product. The government also can't stop the flood of drugs coming over the border from Mexico and they are powerless to stop it from being shipped all over the eastern seaboard.

The reason the War On Drugs has been a dismal failure is based on the same conclusions that the government should have learned with alcohol prohibition nearly a century ago. If people want to get high, they are going to get high no matter how hard you try and stop them. If it is not alcohol, it will be pot. If it is not pot, it will be cocaine. If people cannot get coke, they will figure out a way to blend battery acid and strychnine together with Sudafed and make some other, even more lethal, concoction.

What the War on Drugs has really done is clog prisons, arrest otherwise law-abiding citizens, give illegal aliens something to barter with and waste our damn tax money. I have a friend we will call Al and he is someone you likely know. Al doesn't drink alcohol to excess, he runs a small private business that is totally legal and he has been married to the same woman for the past 30 years. Al only has one vice: He likes to smoke pot. Generally, a little baggie of weed will last Al for well over a month because he generally smokes just a pinch on the front porch before he goes to bed at night. He says the pot relaxes him and helps him sleep.

Even though Al owns multiple acres of land, he is afraid to grow a couple of marijuana plants. If caught, the state could take everything he has away from him. So, instead, Al is forced to deal with people he would not normally deal with to get that little bit of pot. He doesn't want them to see how nice his house is, fearing himself to eventually be a target of a burglary, so he drives from his place 60 miles round trip to get his little baggie of dope. During the trip he sweats the entire time worried what would happen were he pulled over and found to be carrying weed in his vehicle.

Al pays his taxes, employs other people, works hard and is faithful to his wife. Normally, Al would be someone to look up to, but Al is a criminal because he buys and smokes pot. The notion that the federal government would attempt to ban something that grows naturally from the ground would anger someone like George Washington, who was, himself, a hemp farmer. And, yes, they knew the value of hemp as a textile and the effect that smoking hemp had on the human body back in Washington's day. Remember, even Jesus turned water not into fruit juice, but (Someone? Bueller?) wine. The Biblical story of the wedding would not be as compelling had Christ provided V-8 as a drink. Even Christ would likely scoff at banning a weed.

The Libertarians would vote to immediately legalize all drugs and I don't agree with them at all. There is a big difference between marijuana and heroin. However, the vast bureaucracy of the federal government has better things to do than chase after people like Al. As long as an agricultural product is grown and consumed in the same state, then the national government has no jurisdiction under the Constitution. If the people of Georgia decide to legalize pot, then I dare the federal government to come and pry the joint from my dead fingers! Or, well, Al's dead fingers, the stuff makes me paranoid and I don't like that feeling. I find myself paranoid enough knowing the NSA is camped out several miles from my office. However, should I desire to plant a few hemp plants along with my tomatoes and corn, then why should the federal government care?

Like any other agricultural product, should someone decide to grow more marijuana than what is deemed an amount for personal use, the federal government may become involved due to the Interstate Commerce Clause. If anyone is looking for an evangelical argument about gateway drugs, it is not to be found here. More people have died from alcohol than marijuana. Certainly no one wants anyone high on anything sitting behind the wheel of a moving vehicle, but the reasonable person would infer that banning a weed that naturally grows from the ground is an exercise in lunacy.

Marijuana does not have to be processed to create a usable drug as does other substances like cocaine and heroin. Pot can be picked off the bush and smoked in raw form. If this nation had any sense it would allow marijuana to be grown, tax it and be done with it. In the process, ending the ridiculous war on marijuana will free up space in prisons, give the illegal aliens and welfare schemers one less thing to trade with and dismantle a wasteful and expensive bureaucracy. The real ones who benefit from the War on Drugs are the alcohol and tobacco manufacturers. Naturally, they have an army of lobbyists that keep this idiotic policy in place.

The argument here is not suggesting America do away with all of her liberal social programs and regulatory agencies. There were some New Deal ideas such as rural electrification that were massive successes. The Environmental Protection Agency is also an important regulatory mechanism because we all know that if it is cheaper for a factory to dump waste in a waterway rather than treat and dispose of it properly, there would hardly be a river left in the nation that wasn't clogged with sludge. Some federal programs do provide for the general welfare, but the ones that are among the most expensive are the same ones that have accomplished absolutely nothing.

Rather than spending money to chase down and incarcerate the pot smokers in this country, it would be far more right and proper for federal money to be provided to states and municipalities to develop programs like what our landfill employees are doing here in Augusta. Landfills contain mostly organic material. As the material breaks down, it creates methane gas that is harmful to the environment. Rather than burn off the methane, Augusta's solid waste department is looking to capture it and convert it to compressed natural gas. That gas can be used to power city vehicles and public buildings. The gas burns clean, so it is a money saver as well as a green technology. Imagine how many barrels of oil would be saved if every city in America harvested their landfill methane. Doing so across the country would be turning trash into cash. In such a scenario, the federal bureaucracy could certainly help with funding to make such a program universal throughout the nation. However, spending millions of dollars studying how cow farts impact the environment is not only silly, it is expensive and will never lead to powering a vehicle any more than spraying herbicide all over marijuana fields will stop Al from enjoying his evening joint.

All across this nation sit bridges that are not fit for horse and buggy traffic, yet the money that would be available for repairs is instead used for unconstitutional agencies like HUD and unconstitutional laws like the ones banning marijuana. The 10th Amendment should be simple for the federal government to grasp. In plain language, it reads that unless the Constitution specifically allows a law or regulation, then that law or regulation is illegal. Similarly, the General Welfare provision means that anything Congress does to benefit the general welfare must actually benefit the GENERAL welfare and not a select group or segment of society. If one citizen is to get a brand new house for virtually nothing, then all who legally live in America should get one as well. Along the same vein, the Great War on Poverty has done nothing other than deplete the treasury while actually institutionalizing poverty. To compound the felony, your local

89

House Representative won't commit to stop the lunacy, but instead he/she smiles and says he/she is in favor of vague spending cuts. Republicans won't promote legalizing pot because of the fear of ticking off the evangelical Christian arm of their party or pissing in the Wheaties of the liquor distillers. Similarly, no Democrat will vote to force HUD to be accountable because they would lose every one of their welfare roll votes.

Those facts along with the others highlighted in this remarkable little tome reinforce my assertion that true reform must start at the state level and then the states must take it to the federal level. It will not happen any other way.

The federal government is currently this nation's largest employer and that is without factoring in members of the military. That fact should scare the average American. Agencies that have failed at their missions for decades employ thousands of non-essential employees. Even though those same agencies are overstaffed to the rafters, try placing a phone call to them and see if you can get a human being on the line.

The seventh plank of the Contract On The Government does not require anything other than common sense like some of the other planks listed in this book: review and abolish all agencies of the federal government operating in defiance of the 10th Amendment. Those agencies that remain should be forced to account for what they spend. Naturally, this plank would cause federal unemployment to soar and that should be good news to the middle-class taxpayer. Those former federal employees could learn how to pick peaches if necessary and that would take jobs away from the illegal aliens flooding our borders and bringing gang violence to our cities.

One way to immediately begin instituting this plank is for the public to question elected leaders and candidates when they make their blanket "cut spending" promises at their town hall meetings. The next time one of them wags their finger in public and calls themselves a fiscal conservative; the people need to ask what they mean by that statement. What are they going to cut? Will they be cutting funding for important infrastructure improvements or will they cut the mindless bureaucracy? Question the candidates and make them answer before you help place them office. Once they are seated in office, hold them to their word or send them packing on the next go-round.

Conservative pundits love to throw out any phrase with the words "nanny" and "state" included. In the real world though, certain things do need to be mandated by the national government. Losing control of an automobile because you have had too much to drink is an issue the federal government needs to be concerned with since they build and maintain roadways. The public airwaves should be regulated in a manner to allow for free speech but also provide protection from obvious use of obscenity since those airwaves are limited and they cross state lines.

The Federal Bureau of Investigation is also an important national institution. Even though the FBI has had its issues in the past for compiling information on people at the behest of J. Edgar Hoover for his own personal ends, Hoover is long gone and the agency has proven itself more than competent acting as the law enforcement liaison for the several states. Every FBI agent I have ever encountered, and there have been quite a few, act in person like a local Sheriff Investigator much more so than a federal G-Man. They are cops, just at a higher level. If they were not forced to scour the countryside for pot fields, they might actually have time to take an interest in ANIC's tax returns.

Just because the federal government has vastly overstepped its bounds in many areas does not mean that it is not sometimes successful when carrying out its Constitutional duties. It will not be long before broadband service is available from border to border if the national government continues in the direction it is going. Modern children have the job of paying attention in Pre-K and Kindergarten instead of helping run the looms at a factory all thanks to federal child labor laws.

It does not take a lot of searching to find even more examples of where the national government has been successful. There has never been the catastrophic failure of a dam or nuclear fission plant since we began building them. Three Mile Island, the only nuclear crisis we have had so far was a success in that disaster was avoided and a whole host of information was learned about the safe operation of nuclear reactors. Yet, it is the federal bureaucracy that stymied efforts over the years to build more nuclear plants.

The American military is another success story when it comes to the operation of the federal government. If you took away every gadget, device, bit of armor and weaponry from the average American soldier and left him or her out in the middle of the wilderness, he or she would manage to find a way back to your doorstep and be ready to tangle. Despite the power we have vested in the military, never in our history there have been coups or insurrections caused by our military. The same might not be said for the CIA, an agency that has only experienced success in getting Americans killed.

NASA took humanity to the moon, launched the Hubble Telescope and was instrumental in the creation of the International Space Station. Need I say more? Imagine what George Washington would think about when taking a modern tour of the Smithsonian. For a moment, consider what Jefferson might think of the modest collection of books he sold to the government that is today the United States Library of Congress.

America could be building nuclear power reactors in every state that are as safe as the ones that power nearly every major ship in the current American Navy. The American dollar can continue to fund research in the vacuum of space and in the depths of the Oceans because the research performed in those places has brought forth information that benefits humanity. There is no reason why broadband Internet service cannot be available today to rural residents. It should be, and it would benefit the general welfare.

For any of that to happen, both eliminating entire agencies and demanding accountability for the ones that escape the scalpel must happen to pare down the federal government. It has to be the people running for elected office being the ones to articulate which of the federal programs should be eliminated, but I believe I've identified a good road map here. Even though the road map now exists, there is still a major obstacle.

The current nor immediate future elected class is not going to volunteer to serve the particular duty of actually cutting the out of control services that are sucking the treasury dry. The political class will not bring about the seventh plank of the Contract On The Government; the people must bring it about. It must be demanded and the citizens have that right under the First Amendment to make such demands. Americans themselves must take the initiative and force these reforms. What that means is the Tea Parties need to take their rallies to the state capitols such as Atlanta instead of gathering in minor cities like Augusta. If you are now beginning to consider yourself a Washingtonian Constitutionalist, then you might consider it your duty to take a copy of this book to your state capitol and wave the cover in the face of every elected official you encounter. Give them an extra copy if you have one available. You, as a taxpayer, can demand your state representatives execute Washingtonian Constitutionalism in Washington D.C. It is your right to do so under the First Amendment.

If we do not demand these provisions be enacted and our Constitution restored, we will suffer the fate of every major civilization that came before us. If action is not taken, the grand experiment spearheaded by George Washington will simply cease to exist. It will. History is littered with failed governmental models.   Since   you, the reader, have made it this far, you should have no problems listing off to your representatives what agencies you would cut under the seventh plank of the Contract. It really is not rocket science.

Chapter 8.
The Tipping Point And The Abyss

I do not carry nor use credit cards. I pay for what we need with cash and put car repairs before luxuries like a new sofa for the living room. Many years ago, I had a girlfriend get me in a butt-load of trouble using credit in my name. She had some rather expensive tastes. In my world, $145 for a pair of shoes is expensive, but "Mary" wouldn't wear shoes that did not have a name brand embossed on the heel and so just her shoe purchases could go into the thousands of dollars. Looking back, I was a complete moron to ever get involved with this girl, but I did and had to suffer the consequences of my actions.

During the first couple of years of our relationship, Mary's extravagance was not much of a problem. We were both young and the thought of retirement was years away and we were both employed with good jobs. Things changed though when the internet came along and destroyed the hotel marketing industry and I found myself unemployed. While I did not stay jobless for long, my new job only paid a fraction of what my former job paid.

Mary was the one who had always been responsible for paying the bills and managing our shared finances, so I never noticed what was taking place until it was too late. As the savings in the bank were depleted, Mary continued to spend. Being a typical man, I did not pay attention when she came in the house with shopping bags and sometimes Mary was good about discarding the bags quickly so that I would not see them. In hindsight, had I only once checked the trunk of her car, I might have avoided a huge surprise later on.

I must confess, as a typical man, I certainly enjoyed having a very beautiful woman that cared about her appearance at my side. While I did not actively endorse her spending $450 on a dress, the way she looked in those expensive clothes did make me look the other way from the price tags. Reckless spending is one thing when you have the money and quite another when the bank account is not anymore receiving huge infusions of cash. In my case, overnight I went from being a well-paid marketing executive to a flair wearing restaurant server that brought home very little money.

Rather than slow the spending, Mary simply began using my credit card for shopping sprees and expensive lunches. Since I was at work during the day, I didn't know that her spa treatments alone were sending our finances into the abyss. It wasn't long before the minimum payments on the cards meant we couldn't make the rent and Mary had a solution for that, she simply took out a cash advance to cover the funds not in the bank account. Either she didn't realize or didn't care, but cash advances carry a much higher interest rate than a retail purchase, so our credit card bills continued to grow larger and larger until they were out of control.

Finally, Mary was forced to resort to "floating" to keep the bank account out of the red. She would pay one credit card bill with a cash advance from the other credit account. One day I picked up the mail and noticed a credit card bill with a red late notice printed on the envelop and that was the first time over a period of two years that I had actually opened a bill addressed to me and studied the contents.

Reading that first bill was like being punched repeatedly in the gut. I owed over $15,000 to that one creditor. After pouring a stiff drink, I opened more bills and I began to realize that my ship wasn't just on the ice, she had already sunk. By that point, I was not only in debt up to my eyeballs, but I had nothing to show for all the money that had been spent. Several bills, like the power bill, were so far behind that it was amazing that I had never come home to find services to the house cut off for non-payment.

It should come as no surprise that Mary's irresponsibility led to the end of that romance. She packed up her Prada and drifted off into the wind leaving me financially ruined. During those days I was forced to simply turn the ringers off the telephones. Creditors called day and night demanding, cajoling and threatening either I pay up or they would cart away everything I owned. The only problem was I did not own anything other than a eight year old vehicle. I had no savings and did not own a home, but I did have a job. As a consequence, the creditors kept me up at night telling me they would garnish my wages.

During that time, I learned more than just one lesson. First of all, never again would I allow someone else total control over my finances. It was my own laziness that allowed the charade to run its course. I also decided that once I paid off the credit cards, I would be forever done with credit cards. Over the years I have stuck to my guns on both accounts. I would no more stuff a credit card in my wallet than I would a dead fish.

In the Hudson household, we have insurance to cover any imaginable calamity. I squirrel away what I can for retirement and have a little fund that will eventually aid my daughter when she is ready to attend college. But we are steadfast in our belief that credit cards are evil and we simply do not want the temptation they present. What it means for this household is vacations are taken on a budget, restaurant trips are limited and we do not buy things we cannot afford. This is the way most normal private households are run.

Right now, the bills of the federal government are being paid by Mary using the same formula that eventually wrought havoc in my personal life. The government uses the same floating technique to keep cash sitting in the can. As others have pointed out, there is no such thing as a Social Security trust fund. Al Gore never got his "lockbox." The money for Social Security that comes out of every legal paycheck issued in this nation is not locked away for the future use of the individual, but instead spent to pay down another current bill.

The federal government's Mary is not only floating the bills, she continues to spend money she knows she does not have on extravagant items. Mary of the fed is not satisfied with a chicken sandwich from McDonald's for lunch; she has to have Foie de Gras from La Maison Restaurant every single day. Ultimately this country is going to end up in the same situation I found myself in once I finally wised up and kicked Mary to the curb. Only, as so many people have pointed out before, the current bill owed by the American people cannot be eliminated within the lifespan this current generation if the federal government remains at its current size.

Talk radio hosts may sound like the trumpet of Chicken Little doom when they warn listeners that the government is currently spending the paychecks of the next generation, but they are correct. It is hard for the average person to wrap his or her brain around the concept, so I will attempt to condense the warning into a few simple sentences. On my personal level, Mary only drove me around 40 grand into the hole. For many people that amount is petty, but for this little average Joe that worked in a restaurant, it wasn't.

In fact, it took over ten years to pay down that debt and get my good name back without me having to file bankruptcy. It took a lot of sacrifice on my part. It meant for a very long I could not own a house because no one would finance one in my name. When I could actually buy a car, I had to agree to inflated interest rates. For the years I was in college, I chose to put money towards the debt and did not pay the $300 a month I would have normally shelled out for health insurance.

Being massively in debt and financially overextended with a tiny income is a real bitch. Because of the debt, I had to move in with my parents for a short time and that was the least painful part of the story.

To compare my story of Mary with our national debt might seem a bit absurd, however, consider this: at any point during those ten years of paying down debt, as an individual I could have punted and declared bankruptcy. Overnight, many of those debts I struggled under would have vanished had I chose that option and many individuals do take the consequences and file as being broke. Bankruptcy is not possible for a government the size of the United States. Instead, when the day arrives that the assets and income are totally outweighed by interest on the debt and the cost of maintaining operation, the operation will simply cease to exist.

As I pointed out before, extinction is what happened to the Soviet Union. The individual states of that union began to understand they collectively could not pay for Moscow's burden and excesses as a whole any longer and the only way to dissolve much of that debt was to disband entirely. That is precisely what they did and why, on our shores, the Cold War shifted to the War Over Oil which was eventually called the War on Terror.

The Soviets no longer had an empire because they no longer had a treasury to draw from or individual states willing to allow themselves to be mired in debt taken out by a central committee. Please understand, the individual states of the Soviet Union seceded, and they did so because it was the only way forward. No outside force conquered the Soviet Union and in a society that has historically been paternalistic and repressive, there was general and overwhelming cry for liberty.

What happened in the Soviet Union was that after the majority of Warsaw Pact countries declared independence, the Presidents of the three main republics remaining met in a secret conference. With a stroke of a pen, the presidents of Russia, Belarus and Ukraine declared the Soviet Union no longer existed. What that meant was any debt owned by the former union did not exist either. The resignation of Gorbachev was completely symbolic. He could today continue to call himself the President of the USSR, but he would preside over a country with no sovereignty, no military, no land, no assets and no ability to pay him a salary.

According to the Americans for a Balanced Budget Amendment's data, the current figure of the United States national debt stands at around $16 trillion. In the case of Mary and me, there was no way to spend ourselves out of debt and the same law of financial physics applies to the national debt. The government does not have a rich Aunt Edna who will to pony up a few thousand dollars to keep harmony in the family. When people warn that Social Security will not be able to pay out what it owes monthly as the Baby Boomers continue to retire, their warnings are right on the mark. Money is finite; one can't just print it and pass it out. Individuals can't do it without facing arrest, and neither can governments. Remember, physical arrest and cardiac arrest are both forms of arrest. The big old spenders might point out an individual can't print money but the federal government does the equivalent all the time. Their rhetoric is that the government prints the money, therefore they own it. That is simply not true. American money is only as valuable as it is perceived to be by the people to which it is owed.

American money is not backed by anything other than the belief that it is real legal tender. If you look closely to an old Confederate note, it included language actually stating that it was not real. The early Confederate money came with a disclaimer stating it would be worth its face value amount after the war ended. Those notes were not backed in gold or anything other than the confidence of the people trading them at the time. When the Confederate dollar collapsed, so did the Confederacy's war effort and the Confederacy itself. The simple problem is that the more money the government puts into circulation devalues the common currency as a whole. Therefore, you may get $5 more in that Social Security check, but the price of bread goes up $2.75 right along with the raise in the check. While there may be more money out there, the total value of all of the collective money is less. This means that all goods cost more.   The federal government recently announced it was buying millions of dollars worth of its own bonds. I loved how the media announced the decision; they totally sidestepped what the federal government did and reported what happened as ho-hum regular business. What the government did do was start monetizing the debt, and that is something akin to rearranging deck chairs on a ship bound for the bottom. You cannot print money to buy your own debt!   After she realized we were in a terrible financial hole, Mary tried the same floating technique the federal government is attempting now by taking cash advances to pay outstanding bills. What was happening was that our personal income was devalued every time the minimum payments got larger. My paycheck was spread thinner each month.   Mary was working on the assumption that I was a brilliant marketing executive and eventually someone would employ me and we would pull ourselves out of the hole. Only, in reality, I had gone from being a marketing executive to a bartender and she was not able to keep up with the shell game for very long working with the amount of money I was bringing home. We ran harder, but the tipping point eventually came.   The government of this vast country cannot continue to play an economic shell game either; I repeat, you cannot spend your way out of debt. Floating bills back and forth paying a minimum amount still garners mounting interest which makes the bills steeper. To pay a bill with money you create out of nothing simply makes the money you have less valuable and it does not reduce the value of the debt.   The current policy of the national government is to pay only the credit card minimum payment and to borrow more money at the same time hoping a future booming economy might solve the problem and pump more money onto the treasury in the form of more spendable income for the taxpayer. It is a gamble that has continued for decades. Only, when the economy has experienced good fortune in the past, the government has never reined in the spending during those good times and saved up for the eventuality of a downturn. The budget surplus of the Clinton era was a myth. Just because you are able to pay the monthly bills without incurring further debt, if you own thousands of dollars in debt and you can barely pay the interest, you do not have a surplus. What you have in that case is a financial stalemate.

Instead of doing what normal people do and cut up the credit cards, the government and their army of bureaucrats, lobbyists and pundits are simply coming up with new schemes of taxation.

My personal favorite is the one known as the value added tax. This one is very simple. Let's say you start with a bunch of boards, some wire, and a few pieces of ivory. Once the tree is cut, the metal for the wire mined and the elephants killed then each of those things are worth more because they are considered to be recovered raw materials, so they get a little tax added when they are sold. In other words, the tusk is taxed just because it is no longer on the elephant.

Next, the boards are cut and assembled into a casing and sold to a piano manufacturer and naturally the casing is worth more than the raw wood in bulk so the value accrued is then taxed against the piano manufacturer. The process continues with a manufacturer who has paid an extra tax on the wood, the wires, and the ivory and they assemble the final product and sell it to a retailer. Since, of course, the finished piano is worth more than the sum of its individual parts, the retailer pays another tax. All of those little embedded taxes will be ultimately charged to the person who buys that piano for the centerpiece of their living room.

For those still unclear on the scheme, think of a passenger train traveling from New York to Philadelphia. Each passenger pays individually for a ticket, but the train company has to pay a tax at each stop along the line. The ticket price paid up front would naturally become more expensive as the train continued down the line. In the end, just like with the assembly of the piano, it is the consumer that is going to pay more for the product because the product is more expensive to bring to market. And those that argue that this is a consumption tax are using a well thought out income tax alternative to lie to the American people. The VAT would be an additional tax embedded into every item manufactured and sold in America. People would pay income taxes and the VAT at the same time.

In many cases, the VAT is already in place; and this pernicious VAT is not charged because the item grows in value over each step of the manufacturing process, but because of the nature of the item. This is what we all refer to as a "sin" tax.

My brother and I opened up a liquor store thinking that such a business model would be recession proof. We found the perfect location, conducted marketing studies on what the people in our geographic area enjoyed drinking the most and designed a beautiful showroom to sell off our wares. The one thing we didn't take into account was just how often the government would be sticking its hand in our till.

Even though a bottle of liquor does not change at all from the factory to the consumer, it is taxed every stop along the way. When a bottle leaves the factory it is taxed by the federal government. For the privilege of entering the state where it will be sold, the state levies a tax to the distributor. When the distributor sells to the retailer, another tax is levied. Finally, when the retailer sells the product to the consumer, yet another 8 or so percent is added before the bottle leaves the building. You would think that would be close to the end of the taxation, but it is not.

Liquor stores pay the normal startup costs of any business, but because the product being sold is state regulated there are several other embedded costs in the form of taxes and fees. Liquor stores pay for a state and a local license to sell liquor and it only one little mistake to have that license revoked for 10 years, effectively putting the store out of business.

State Revenue Department individuals know that they do not have to be reasonable to the license holder as they have them by the balls. Our store had a dedicated bookkeeper who was Johnny-on-the-spot with keeping track of our sales tax collection and making sure the state got their money on time. So, you can imagine my shock when I received a penalty bill for non-payment of the state sales tax.

What was even more shocking and confusing was the document presented to me in person by some little bubble-headed bleach blonde with a badge was that the document stated I was being fined $2,000 for owing $0.00. No, you read that right, I was being fined for owing nothing.

I called the Revenue Department in Atlanta and was told to disregard the document. The nice lady explained that the state was converting to a new computer system and they were busy working out the bugs. A few weeks later the little bubble-head returned and this time she presented a demand for payment along with interest and further penalties. When I told her that I had spoken with the folks in Atlanta, she became defiant and responded that the people in Atlanta didn't know what was going on and I should have never called them. The rest of our conversation went like this:

"But this document says I am being fined for non-payment of zero dollars and zero cents."

"That's right."

"So, I paid the sales tax on time."

"That's right."

"Then why are you fining me for paying my taxes on time?"

"Because the payment wasn't entered into the system correctly."

"What system?"

"Our system."

"So, let me get this straight, you are fining me for a mistake made on your end."

"That pretty much sums it up."

She ended the conversation by telling me that I had two choices. I could pay the penalty or request a hearing in Atlanta, but if I did not pay up immediately, my license would be temporarily suspended until the hearing date. Needless to say, I paid the fine.

Several weeks after my run-in with "Tabitha," I received another bill in the mail, this time from the local government. This time it was a property tax bill on my inventory, equipment and fixtures. My mouth dropped to the floor. I had already paid tax multiple times on the inventory and now they were taxing me for not selling it! They were also taxing me for the chandelier that hung from the ceiling even though I paid sales tax when I bought it.

After a year and a half of this bullshit, my brother and I reevaluated the situation. It was clear that between sales tax, property tax, licenses, fees, inspection costs and fines that we would never be able to make any money. Our store sat just blocks from the Augusta National golf course and was a mad house during the Masters® Tournament week, but all the foot traffic in the world was not going to help when our mark-up was on average 25% and a good 10% of that went back to the government.

My brother and I got out of the retail business not because we didn't enjoy the experience, but because we were being taxed and fined out of business. The lesson we learned is one that virtually every small business learns and it is no wonder that small businesses are almost becoming a rarity. My personal experience should illustrate that the government does not have a problem collecting money. The problem is not revenue collection but the government's inability to stop spending more than they take in.

In the meantime, to overcome the revenue versus spending deficit, the government is printing more money. This means the average value of the dollar declines at a faster rate than the tax's monetary value does and therefore prices of all goods increase and so do the taxes. In our case, the government is attempting to introduce even more money on loan as a "stimulus" while paying the minimum credit card payment, floating money from account to account, and printing cash out of thin air. That scheme worked real well in Romania if you recall.

Furthermore, if you hated seeing that little "made in the USA" symbol on products back in the good old days, the value added tax will ensure you never have to see it on a label again in your lifetime. The government's waste and over burdensome taxes have already driven most manufacturing overseas and this little scheme will send the rest away to Mexico and China.

Governments that came before the United States and many after its creation have learned the hard lesson that financial instability due to massive taxation of a few and the promise of benefits for all leads to an insurmountable burden. Attempting to create empire with the same internal structure of financial instability, according to history, always leads to disaster. Anyone who argues that America has not become an empire is a fool. Just because this country does not have colonies does not mean that American influence across the globe rises to the level of empire status. Oh, wait, we do have colonies, one is called American Samoa and there is another one called Puerto Rico. The United States has become an empire by any reasonable definition.

Empires rise and empires fall. Throughout history we can clearly see the reason empires fall is due to the eventual inability for the empire to fund itself.

The reason you are likely reading this book is because you are among the masses that are tired of the government finding sneaky new ways to tax citizens without offering any checks on its own spending. You may have noticed that your net income remains stagnant while the taxes as well of the cost of goods continue to rise. It may be that you have also come around to the realization that the government's Mary is going to continue to float around her limited income from account to account so that she may continue the lifestyle she has become accustomed to and the spending habits she expects to remain forever unchanged. You may be among the masses that are beginning to understand what Mary has been doing behind your back and understand it was all being done at your expense because she never really cared about you in the first place. If any of those thoughts have crossed your mind, then you know already that the eighth plank of The Contract On The Government is one of the initiatives described here that needs to be enacted immediately.

The eighth plank of The Contract On The Government is the inclusion of a Constitutional Balanced Budget Amendment. We the people must take the credit card away from the government and tell Mary to go find herself another chump to screw over and leave penniless. When taken together with the other planks of the Contract, an amendment that forces the ink to be black on the current year's books would actually put the country on the path to unseen prosperity within a matter of years.

All the other fiscal solutions of this Contract taken together with a Balanced Budget Amendment would replenish the treasury and will manage to draw down the debt by the time the next generation steps up to draw Social Security. That is, should that next generation decide Social Security is still a necessary program.

It must also be noted that after years of economic malaise, the United States has found itself sitting on vast reservoirs of oil in Montana. We already knew about the oil in Alaska and the trick is how to export it out. Even though the process of fracking has been the subject of controversy, the truth is we have more energy reserves here on the homeland than we ever realized before. We have the opportunity to become independent of OPEC in the coming years. However, if history is any guide, the political class will use the coming energy boom as a means to generate positive headlines and will continue to spend like they do today. When the energy boom begins to wane as it surely will, the country will be in an even worse position than it is right now. In fact, we will have wasted the opportunity and only staved off going over a real financial cliff.

George Washington's first order of business as president was to pay off the United States debt to France and he did it with limited resources. George Washington also believed power flowed from the consent of the governed to the government. Washington must have also been keenly aware that phrase declaring consent was loaded to be misinterpreted to mean consent of the majority. He knew that if a poll were taken in America, there would likely never have been a revolution. Therefore, through his writings we can see that he felt the emerging nation with a capitol named in his honor would have to be based on realistic principles set into a framework of protocol. That protocol is no longer being followed by the leaders of this nation; in fact many of this country's leaders have open disdain for Washington and his clearly articulated ideals.

Woodrow Wilson was the first American president to say that the Constitution had become irrelevant and the men after him continued to craft and enforce law based on precedent and not what might actually be written in the founding document. The changing of the rules while in the midst of playing the game has extended to everything from warfare to finance.

As a military man, Washington understood only a tight and balanced chain of command and command structure could make for a successful army and he applied those structural ideals as both General of the Continental Army, participant architect of the Constitution and later as civilian President. In helping form the nation, Washington and his contemporaries not only designed a system that could not fall under military dictatorship easily, but one that could also withstand the pressures of the democratic ideals that could lead to tyranny of the other form.

One of the biggest things Washington remained concerned with as President was paying down the war debt from the Revolution and he would likely be appalled to see the national debt as it stands today. We must remember that in Washington's day, no money in the treasury meant no money for biscuits and none of which to buy grain for the horses. Back then, money actually had value backed by silver and gold. Today, our money is backed only by the country of China.

A Constitutional amendment to limit Congress's spending power in the form of a forced balanced budget along with a 10% across the board reduction of the federal budget is the starting point. That follows the necessary changes in the size and scope of the federal bureaucracy by simply adhering to the 10th Amendment. Those actions combined with the presidents line item veto power and putting the Senate back in place representing the states will move this nation immediately back towards the ideals of Washingtonian Constitutionalism and avoid the train wreck Cicero warned Rome of centuries ago. The empire must be placed back under the control of the tax payers that fund its ability to govern.

Establishing control of the national financial mess is the most important aspect of the Contract On The Government. As I have stated over and again, empires throughout history have collapsed due to finances. The United States is now an empire and we are about to collapse. It won't happen this year or maybe in the next decade, but the tipping point will eventually come. Remember, gravity is a law.

It is time to hit the "reset" button or face the looming threat that our children will grow up to inherit. Like the average household, America must pay the water bill and electricity bill and stop indulging in luxuries. If that means more children will starve overseas without our aid, then so be it. Likewise, if it means some Americans starve in the process, then we must allow for that eventuality. However, in this nation, the only ones who will starve under these much needed reforms are the people who refuse to be responsible individuals. They will starve because they choose to.

If reigning in the federal government's ability to tax the workers and then give the money to the slackers of society means that some homeless person may die, then I must say it is better for one fool to perish in drowning waters than for the entire community perish trying to save him. The young, the elderly, the chronically ill, and the physically handicapped should be taken care of with compassion and love. Everybody else needs to get a damn job.

Could it mean that stopping federal aid to belligerent countries might cause regional destabilization and lead to war? Yes, it could. But if any country at this point in the modern world decided to seriously light one of those powder kegs, the result would be Armageddon and they all know that. Countries such as Iran and North Korea enjoy playing the game they are playing with the world. After all, it has been profitable for them for decades, so why not just let it continue is their policy.

What about the oil?

Scientists found and put together the means for energy alternatives years ago. The methane to natural gas alternative described earlier could heat homes thereby reducing oil. Everyone doesn't have to have a hotrod; electric cars are already a reality and the hybrid technologies will only get better. Besides, we have oil sitting under American soil and resting off of her shores. We have vast reserves already here in this country. Therefore, this country in a matter of years can be in a position to tell the Arabs to eat their fucking oil and be done with it.

Cutting federal spending means taking some very painful steps on all fronts, but it must be done. Out of all the planks in the Contract On The Government, this one truly controls the health of the Republic and must be handled with the same vigor that the honest shop owner displays when faced with massive debt and discovering an employee stealing from the till. It is time to tell Mary that the shell game is over. An amendment must be passed that requires a balanced operating budget of the federal government each year. The only other alternative is to face the abyss head on with blinders as we are doing today and the outcome will be that the United States will wither and slowly disappear from the face of planet Earth.

In 2008, the company I worked for found itself in a pickle. We had eight radio stations operating out of our building and of those eight stations, only two were really profitable. WGAC and WKXC were selling ads like crazy, but we could not give away airtime on stations like "Bob FM" and "95 Rock." The company decided that layoffs were necessary and the cuts were made throughout the building. I found myself doing traffic reports in the morning as an addition to my reporter duties. The man who was our staff meteorologist pulled a traffic reporting shift in the afternoon. Some of our talk show hosts pulled double time acting as producers for other shows and everyone that escaped the layoffs agreed to a five percent pay cut and guess what happened?

We became a stronger company. We became better at doing our jobs and the radio company escaped going into bankruptcy. All of the underperforming formats remained on the air, but we learned how to continue to broadcast with less people and less resources. Our sales people bundled advertising together to support the lesser listened to stations and while during the process a lot of people lost their jobs, ultimately the company survived. We basically cut the 10% of fat on our bellies and grew to be a lean machine.

It is now a known fact that had the leadership on the bridge of the R.M.S. Titanic upon spotting the iceberg simply reversed the engines and kept course, the ship would not have foundered. To be sure, the impact would have been terrible. Every one person on the ship would have been violently thrown about and the ones in forward compartments would have died on impact. The bow would have crumpled into a mass of wrecked steel, but the ship would have stayed afloat. Instead, the bridge attempted a maneuver that doomed the liner. They found out that 46,000 ton ship will not turn on a dime and they created a bigger tragedy by being reactive instead of being proactive when facing an unavoidable crash.   Our national government is racing towards that berg and we are going to hit it with a certainty. How we hit the ice is now up to us. We can ram that motherfucker and save the vessel or we can graze it and slowly go down with it into the icy waters. The choice is up to us, the People.

I have read where several economists have come forward to say that ending the federal deficit cannot be managed without ending virtually all governmental spending. According to these "economists," it would take multiple generations to pay off the national debt even if the government ended every program that cost money tomorrow. Do not believe what these people are telling you. They can rearrange the deck chairs all they want; I am putting on a life preserver and preparing to jump overboard if the moment of necessity approaches while the so-called experts are hiding out in the salon drinking a final round hoping a lifeboat will be waiting for them. The economists that say we should continue to allow the federal government to spend itself into oblivion are part of the problem. They don't want you to be alarmed, because if you are alarmed then you might take action.

Not only do I want you to be alarmed, I want you to be angry. Hopefully, your anger will spur you into action. Hopefully you will demand the reforms we must have to survive even if it means you will share in some of the immediate suffering.

A 10% reduction of the federal budget will hurt everyone temporarily, but along with the other planks of The Contract On The Government, it will indeed keep the ship afloat. That scenario is what we want to have happen. Hit the iceberg, I say. Hit it and then attend to the wounded as needed.

It is true that curbing domestic welfare alone will only be a drop in the bucket when it comes to paying down the deficit. The same can be said about curtailing foreign aid and enforcing 10th Amendment to reign in the federal bureaucracy if those measures are taken independently and alone. When combined, though, we are talking about cutting out trillions of dollars that are currently being bled from the treasury.

The 8th plank of the Contract on the Government is the inclusion of a balanced budget amendment and the further commitment to a 10% across the board reduction in all federal spending at the Congressional level over the course of five years and that includes a cut in the salaries of Congress.

In 2013, almost everyone in government howled at the "sequester" and made every attempt to scare the public into thinking that even the most minor of cuts to the budget would cause planes to fall out of the sky and the Earth to tremble. What was not explained to the public was that the so-called sequester had nothing to do with cutting the budget, what it did was prevent spending increases for the next year. So the government was spending the same amount of money it spent the year before, but because it did not get an extra bucket of slop thrown into the trough, the decision was made to cancel White House tours and furlough air traffic controllers.

Former Speaker of the House, Nancy Pelosi, had the gall to claim that the draconian sequestration caused her to have to cancel a trip to visit American troops abroad on Mother's Day. This is the same woman who forced the taxpayers to fund her weekly trips from Washington D.C. to California on a jumbo jet loaded up with booze for her and her staff. This is the same woman who said of the Obama health care bill that Congress needed to go ahead and pass the legislation so everyone could find out what was in the bill! If the voters in California want to keep electing this brainless moron, then fine, but the rest of us need to elect people who are going to go to Washington and do our bidding and relegate her to just one vote in the House.

If a 10% across the board cut means Nancy has to stay home with her kids on Mother's Day, then no one should have a problem with making the cuts. As I have stated many times in this book, we the People need to demand this occur. If it means rallying at the state capitols waving this book in the face of every state representative, then that is exactly what we the People need to do. We must remember, Congress is never going to vote to cut their own budget. Congress is never going to agree on their own to end the practice of earmarks. Congress will never agree to slash their own salaries and reduce the size of their staffs. It will have to be the state governments that force these needed changes at the threatened point of a bayonet. I say that figuratively speaking, of course.

You and I do not have the right to mark a big zero on our tax return and mail it to the IRS. Just because we are forced to pay does not mean we should be forced to sit and watch as Congress spends our money on frivolous studies, vanity projects, arms to hostile nations and cell phones to the homeless. When a private individual forces someone to give them the money out of their wallet, we call that robbery; when the government does it, we call it tyranny.

At the time of this writing, it has been over three years since the Senate even passed a budget. It is time the government be forced to pass a budget and then balance the books.

Chapter 9.
The Scourge of Racism

One of the scariest moments of my life was when I stood in front of an audience made up almost exclusively of black teenagers and preceded to tell them that slavery was a good thing when it began. Some of the fellows in the audience looked like they were ready to rip my head from my shoulders after I first dropped that little nugget of information as a declaratory sentence. Thankfully, they allowed me to explain myself.

The talk was part of a lecture series co-sponsored by the Richmond County, Georgia school system that had me discussing the history of slavery and segregation with kids that have historically been given only a portion of the story. Make no mistake, I am not an apologist for slavery, but I feel that everyone needs an unvarnished understanding of what it was and what it was not if we are to put racism behind us and continue to band ourselves together.

There was a far greater evil than slavery that occurred on American soil, and that evil was institutionalized segregation.

Normally, the topics of racism, slavery and segregation would have no place in a book about Constitutional amendments and fiscal conservatism. To that end I am sure even the vaunted Rev. Al Sharpton would agree. Then again, what am I saying is, in Sharpton's mind and those of his followers, even the very air we all breathe is tainted with racist undercurrents and the fact people believe this impacts our government and its day to day workings.

At the onset of writing this book, I did not plan on addressing the societal issue of racism. However after further reflection, I believe that the American people must at long last address the wrongs perpetrated against the black citizens of this country. The Contract On The Government is useless if people continue to vote on candidates based on the color of their skin and many times that is exactly what happens.

Some may question my decision to address racism predicated on the fact this book is about Washingtonian Constitutionalism and Washington was known to have been a slaveholder. It may even seem a bit hypocritical. But there is more to the Washington slavery story than is generally covered in textbooks.

George Washington was among a group of men that believed slavery to be an immoral and unsustainable practice. "Historians," when writing about the first President, rarely include the fact that he considered the institution of slavery to be one of the sins visited upon the colonies by King George III. Since it does not fit the model of a paternalistic, misogynist, racist old white guy, modern students are generally not told that Washington was the only slave holding President to free all of his slaves upon his death. And it certainly is not reported that Washington's will stipulated that his estate would continue to take care of his former slaves until their deaths.

Fast forward to the modern world and we find racial issues continuing to dominate decision making when it comes to public policy and that filters down to elections. There is a large percentage of Americans who cast their ballots solely on the color of a candidate's skin as opposed to the content of the nominee's character. Understand that it is not only Barak Obama who made his way into the White House using race as a playing card, there have been plenty of white folks elected because the other fellow running was black. The uneasiness of the races has had a detrimental effect on every aspect of this nation's collective psyche. All of this started not with the end of slavery, but with the beginning of segregation.

The issue of the Framers owning slaves must be addressed. It is true that many of them did participate in slavery and it is also true that slavery was the backbone of the agricultural and skilled artisan body of early America. Yet, again, there is more to the story. After slavery, there was an evolution that learned men (and women) failed to recognize as it progressed and that progression led to racist evil on both sides of the color line.

In the local area here of Augusta, we actually had a candidate campaign and almost win an election by going around and telling everyone he deserved to win because that particular seat on the city commission belonged to a black person. This fellow basically told voters never mind he had an abysmal track record in public service and that he had once physically beaten a local community activist, who was half his size, to the ground at a public meeting; rather he very clearly articulated that voters should pick him because of his skin color.

In the same vein, no one should forget that before Strom Thurmond had his change of heart, he ran for president under the banner of "Segregation forever." The real racists out there use the argument on both sides that the Framers held slaves. For some, that makes slavery legitimate in their minds, and others see it as an opportunity to continue trying to make the Framers irrelevant.

I told the kids who attended my lecture that slavery, like many human endeavors gone wrong, was beneficial to everyone who practiced it in the beginning. There were people who wished to travel to the New World, but lacked the means to do so. Ships of the era were rickety and dangerous and transatlantic fare was extremely expensive. So along comes the concept of indentured servitude.

The way it worked was a planter or skilled artisan in America would pay the travel expenses for an individual in exchange for about 7 years of service from the individual. Generally, the individual would not only get the travel expenses paid, but he would be apprenticed in a trade almost guaranteeing him a successful life if he applied himself during the years he agreed to servitude. The concept was more being offered job security for braving the high seas instead of bondage. This arrangement was beneficial to both parties and everything worked out well until some bright bulb had the idea to start kidnapping Africans and forcing them into what became known as the "peculiar institution."

Not only were white Europeans complicit in the kidnapping scheme, there were plenty of Africans on the continent willing to help. When a tribal war occurred, men and women on the losing side were rounded up and sold off. What better way to get rid of your enemies than to sell them to the Dutch! And hence, the tradition of bondage began in the southernmost colonies that would later become an issue that eventually had to be settled with bloodshed.

The Framers of the Constitution knew slavery was morally wrong, even as some of them participated in the institution. It is sad that they likely did not foresee the great fracture slavery would cause in later generations. In the early drafts of the Declaration Of Independence, Thomas Jefferson wanted to include language blaming the King of England for forcing slavery on the colonies. That language was removed at the demand of the southern slaveholders.

Historic records make it clear that those white, paternalistic men we call the Framers understood that slavery was an economic system that would eventually collapse on its own. The transatlantic slave trade was later halted and America began her path to the slow but sure end of the institution. Under the guise of states' rights, southern slave owners continued to try to keep the institution alive fearing sudden economic collapse and the situation deteriorated until it finally led to war. Plenty of people will tell you the Civil War was about tariffs and trade. Southerners to this day cling to the argument that the conflict was about states' rights. The war was, at its core, about states' rights: the right of states to allow slavery. It is just that simple, otherwise there would have not been all the compromises and hand wringing over which new state admitted to the union would be free and which one would allow slaves. In the years leading up to the war, states themselves were being let into the union based on their slave status in an effort to maintain the uneasy balance.

Later, Lincoln would kick off what became the revisionist history line by mentioning that the war was not about slavery at all and the shrewd politician in him did that only to placate the masses of Northerners who thought slavery was none of their business and no reason for America to go to war with itself. But Lincoln knew otherwise. Upon meeting Harriet Beecher Stowe, author of Uncle Tom's Cabin, Lincoln is reported to have said "is this the little woman who wrote the book that made this Great War?"

White men were not the only ones who participated in owning slaves. Many black men fought on the side of the Confederacy out of their own free will and there were also many black men in the South who owned slaves out of their own free will. The claim that black men only bought family members to free them is absolutely not true. I have seen records of black people buying other black people who were in no way blood related to each other. According to the records, there is no indication that many of those black slave owners freed their property once the transaction was made. The bottom line is that slavery was the reality of the times and, unfortunately, the way of life.

The Civil War was a long time in coming; the seeds had been sown since the time of the Revolution. The tensions that finally boiled over were the clash of ideas. Would America be an industrial giant of free citizens or allow for an agrarian economic model based on the use of a slave workforce existing within its borders? It was a question that tragically could not be answered by compromise.

Yet, the compromises and political juggling continued well into the war. It must be noted that President Lincoln, the Great Emancipator, never emancipated anyone. That fact is incontestably true. Lincoln spent his entire career faced with the mess of slavery. At each point in his political career, he treaded lightly, leaning on his knowledge of the law. As we study the brilliance of the men who cobbled this country together after the Revolution, Lincoln must be included in the bunch for drafting a document that said everything, but virtually did nothing at the time it was released to the public.

The language of the Emancipation Proclamation is a polished genius piece of legalese not for what it did, but for what it did not do. It did not free anyone. The Proclamation freed only the slaves in the rebellious states meaning no one had standing to sue over the matter in the Supreme Court, not even Union states that allowed slave-holding since the Proclamation did not apply to them.

Lincoln knew what he was doing when he issued the Proclamation and he intended it to become the law of the land after the war. Eventually the Proclamation did nail the final nail in the coffin of slavery but it began as a document with a flurry of meaningful and sincere, yet unenforceable words. It would take the continued use of bullets to enforce those words and end slavery once and for all. It is ironic and sad that one of the last bullets fired in the conflict struck the man from whose pen created the sentences that are considered sacred to Americans of African heritage.

What happened after the dust of the Civil War settled was far worse than slavery as institutionalized slavery turned into institutionalized segregation. I explained to the high school kids that under slavery, an owner had a vested interest in keeping his property healthy and happy. Naturally, there was abuse and that has been well documented, but the pure raw fact is that most master-slave relations were that of co-existence as extended family. Indeed, sometimes, as in Thomas Jefferson's case, it was an intimate family relationship that developed closely and begat offspring. There is no doubt in my mind that Jefferson was in love with Sally Hemmings.

Segregation was worse, far worse in many ways, than slavery because it made emancipation a hardship rather than a victory. Under the segregationist institution model, the black population as a whole was free, but completely left to fend for themselves. The whole 40 acres and a mule promise never happened for one reason: it was never actually promised to anyone. Former slaves not only missed getting a consolation prize for generations of forced labor, but they found themselves battling a system that was by law set against them. Forced bondage became forced poverty. The cycle of evil begat more evil and things continued to get worse for people of color.

Hospitals would not treat blacks appropriately, theaters and motels denied them service and the fact they had to contend with segregated water fountains was the least of the worries of the average black person. Black people living under Southern segregation were leery of the white person they encountered on the street and they were downright terrified of the police. Blacks were treated as an unwanted and disgusting segment of society by whites who believed they neither deserved nor could even understand the concept of civil rights. Whites of the time cursed openly that Abraham Lincoln should have rounded up all of slaves and sent them back to Africa before unleashing them as free men upon a genteel society. What they weren't taught in school was that Lincoln considered that notion and labored for a way to make it happen until he realized it was an absolute impossibility.

Under legal segregation, blacks were considered a scourge not fit for polite company unless she was serving pie along with the mint juleps and keeping her opinions and thoughts to herself. When a black person did try to assimilate and better himself, he was derided as being 'uppity.' One of the most popular jokes of the time was "what is the difference between a nigger and dog shit?" The answer and punch line was "dog shit eventually turns white and stops stinking."

Real funny, I know.

It did not matter that George Washington Carver was a genius; he was also a black and that made him less than human to the white establishment. It did not matter that it was black men and women that bravely helped settle and tame the western portions of this country. A man could be a black cowboy, but he was still black, a sub human in the eyes of many whites. Adolescent black boys were warned by their mothers not to make eye contact with white girls, lest they might find themselves the victim of a lynch mob. A lynching in the South was routinely followed by a picnic - now how sick is that?

We must explore who was minding the store when segregation became a state sponsored legal affair. That man would be none other than former Augusta resident Thomas Woodrow Wilson. It is important to take Tommy Wilson's early life in context when studying his actions from the Oval Office in this matter. Tommy Wilson's father was a Presbyterian minister who preached at the local church in downtown Augusta. Joseph Ruggles Wilson was also the man who wrote the sermon considered to be the definitive Biblical defense of slavery prior to the Civil War.

Using the book of Ephesians as a guide, Joseph Wilson contended that God set up the structure that some men would be subservient to others and it was the Godly duty of the slave to obey his master. It is important to note that young Wilson grew up in a southern city that was very cosmopolitan when compared to the standards of the time.

There was a large free black population in Augusta during the antebellum days. Those free blacks living in Springfield Village within walking distance of Wilson's boyhood home were skilled artisans. They were literate and many were very gifted orators. When young Wilson did encounter a person of bondage he would have noticed that they were dressed well, as if they themselves were rich.

Only the richest of people living in Augusta owned slaves during that period. Naturally, when the woman of a slave-holding house would send her servant to the market, she would make sure that servant was dressed properly. Therefore, Wilson would likely have never seen the abuses that occurred on the rural plantations, but indeed he should have known that free black men were responsible for building Augusta's greatest technological and engineering triumph, the Augusta Canal.

It is likely that in Wilson's mind, blacks were great laborers but not great thinkers. He would have followed his father's rationale that blacks were created by God to be subservient to whites if he was to be a good son. By all accounts, Tommy was a good son and a great scholar as well. Based on his example, we can reasonably infer that being a good son and a great scholar does not itself make a great leader. It is quite likely that Woodrow Wilson was educated beyond his intelligence.

The mindset that all-was-well in the South accompanied Wilson to the White House. He and his advisers knew of the lynching taking place, the poll taxes and the segregated restrooms yet they declined to act and put a stop to any of it.

Wilson's childhood indoctrination likely led him to be predisposed to thinking exactly what his father preached from the pulpit, that blacks were inferior and therefore had to be controlled. As long as tempers remained cool in the south, Wilson the Great Progressive just did not care how black people were treated because only a small portion of them in the south could vote for him anyway. As noted in this book, he was far more concerned with meddling in European affairs and establishing the legacy for himself as the man who made the world a grand democracy. The plight of the average black person meant nothing to him.

Unfortunately for the black population of the time, no other president gave much of a care to the rights of blacks. It wasn't until those people we now regard as heroes stood up and demanded they be treated equally in accordance to the Constitution that changes began to take place. Martin Luther King Jr. did more to heal the racial divide than all the Presidents in office combined during his short lifetime.

In many southern cities during Segregation, black people could not buy liquor or operate a dance hall without severe restrictions. Police shot blacks dead and justified their actions by saying the "mad negro" was hopped up on cocaine. Blacks were denied entrance into universities, could order lunch and sit at the counter only in black-owned restaurants, and were routinely denied their basic civil rights by juries and judges.

This all culminated into the period of time when thinkers such as Martin Luther King Jr. and others began asking, is it better to be a slave to a man, or a slave to the system? In either situation, one is denied the basic tenet that Thomas Jefferson so eloquently wrote as a God given right to the pursuit of happiness. Thankfully, Dr. King was wise to understand that violence was not the answer to the problem.

In the 1960's, a young Augusta lady and her husband saved their modest earnings intending to go into business for themselves. Lee and Betty Beard lived under the system of segregation, but had managed to do well in life despite the restrictions. They decided they wanted to buy a package liquor store in downtown Augusta. The store was on the market for sale, but the owner had made it clear that he would not sell the store to Coloreds.

According to Ms. Beard, she and her husband had to find a white broker to buy the business for them, at a commission of course, to be able to complete the transaction. Even once the business was in their hands and operating well, it still caused plenty of people in Augusta to be concerned that a couple of Negros had their hands on that much alcohol. Betty and Lee were treated more disrespectfully than anyone living in the post Civil Rights era can imagine.

Betty and Lee would go on to get involved in public service, both were eventually elected as commissioners of the Augusta government. Neither of them forgot the slights of the past and both of them brought their own form of racism and bigotry into the public venue. Only, they came into office at a point in time when whites had realized that the actions of the previous generations were wrong and at times evil. The tide, so to speak, had changed with the arrival of a younger political generation that was not blinded by racism. Rather than embrace the change in thinking, the Beards remained mired in the old school. Sometimes, I find it very hard to blame them. In fact, I really don't blame them at all.

The Beards, as elected officials, were hell-bent on avenging the slights they suffered as young adults. Behind the scenes, Lee shook down government contractors forcing them to use "minority owned" companies that were little more than sham operations. These subcontractors would bill the local government far over what would be a normal price for the work they were contracted to complete. Employees of the government were hired and fired on a tit-for-tat racial basis. If a black were to lose a job, it meant a white had to go as well and vice-versa. If a black person was fired, it was expected that another black person would fill the position regardless of that applicants qualifications.

When the city of Augusta consolidated with the county of Richmond in 1996, the city charter itself was designed to give equal control to the black and white power structures. What that created was chaos and corruption on both sides of the color spectrum. Nearly every vote held by the elected body fell along racial lines. The arrangement led to stagnation and ultimately wasted tons of tax money and it went on for years and years.

When Lee died, Betty assumed his political office and continued his policies. She, along with her cronies, would shake down companies with business pending before the city by demanding "donations" to her favorite charities. Her downfall came when she forced a company to provide a "donation" that eventually went to a personal friend and city employee so that person could have gastric by-pass surgery, commonly called the stomach staple procedure. Other business people came forward and told tales of shakedowns and it was exposed that Augusta was a corrupt and unfriendly place to attempt to conduct business. Betty ended taking the blame.

Lee Beard died with his reputation intact, but Betty was forced to retire in humiliation for her actions as a public official. However, to be fair to Betty, she did nothing against another person that was once not forced upon her. The bigotry shown to her as a young woman was simply returned to others once she gained the same amount of power that people once had over her.

Another rather opposite story that has recently surfaced regards a now former official with the United States Department Of Agriculture, Sheryl Sherrod. The week before the national news story surfaced, I interviewed Sherrod for a news story about rural broadband service being installed in counties throughout Georgia. During the interview, Sherrod came across as someone committed to the modern equivalent of government sponsored rural electrification of the 1930's.

Sherrod was excited her agency was bringing broadband service to school children and business owners in places like Lincoln County that had only dial-up Internet service. Never once did I detect a tone of racism in her voice during the interview. Just the opposite, she was a bureaucrat that seemed to understand her job, liked her job and was willing to tell the press all about the important work she and her agency were doing for the general welfare of the people.

Imagine my surprise a week later seeing Sherrod's name in the national headlines after she apparently confessed to being a bigot.

From the WGAC news center office, I followed the story as it unfolded thinking the whole time that there must be more to the story. I was right. The White House forced her resignation as head of the Department of Rural Development over comments she had made at a NAACP meeting. But there was more to the videotape than was originally shown in the national press. Her full commentary was slow to emerge compared to the original sound-bite. The Obama Administration and some conservative commentators ended up with egg on their faces once the full story came to light.

The final analysis of the story showed that Sherrod was speaking of racial reconciliation at that NAACP meeting. She told a personal story of how she reacted as a black woman to a white man she felt was acting condescending towards her as he was asking for her help in her official capacity. The event had taken place 24 years in the past. What was a story about how this woman had grown and learned from her mistakes was at first presented as the exact opposite by many members of the national press. The original sound bite had her saying she did not give the white farmer the "full force" of her official ability to help when he was in need.

Upon further review, the entire speech Sherrod gave was really about how she made that snap judgment because, as a black woman, she felt the farmer was acting in a superior manner even though he was the one who needed her help. She told the crowd she had always regretted what she had done on that day and she had made amends with the farmer. Later, the farmer's widow backed Sherrod's story. As it turned out, Sheryl Sherrod did help save the farm.

The story of Shirley Sherrod should stand as a symbol of how far we have come as a people who can lay aside the bigotry of the past and move forward understanding ourselves as being people who can help each other regardless of skin tone. We are a people with a common goal and that goal is to embrace everyone in the American family and mend the issues that threaten to destroy this country.

But first, before we move forward with fiscal and social reform, we must confront what occurred in the past.

Were it not for the racial unrest in the country, no one would likely recognize the name Charles Manson. Actress Sharon Tate might today be an aging Hollywood name and not known as the victim of a man wanting to start a brutal race war. It was the racial backlash in the 1960's against the white establishment Manson thought he saw a race war coming and that thought eventually sent him on a killing rampage. Manson himself is a racist who professed to his "family" that when the great race war was over that black people would realize they were too stupid to rule America and so they would pick him as their leader. In 1969, when "Helter Skelter" had not begun on its own, Manson commented to his following that the blacks were too timid to start the war and it was up to the family to get the ball rolling. The result of Manson's racism was a massacre that destroyed countless lives.

Normally, people do not riot in the streets for the sheer fun of rioting. In the early 1970's, there was a riot that occurred in Augusta and it, like other riots across the nation, was the culmination of a group of people so fed up with the establishment's practices that they felt the need to take their grievances to the streets. In this city, all it took was a tiny spark to set off a local civil war. People were killed in the Augusta riots and it took decades for the jagged wounds created by that event to begin to heal.

Thanks to Martin Luther King Jr., James Brown and scores of others, black and white, those dark days passed with black people coming out from the wilderness with pride in the way they had managed to topple the establishment with calm peaceful determination.

After decades of racial politics, people of all colors here in my city are coming together and saying we have had enough of the hate. We have had enough of the corruption, the uneasiness and the mistrust. The citizens of Augusta know that the only path forward is to sit at the same table, break bread with one another and solve our problems together. Our intention now as a city is to be an example to the rest of the nation.

In Augusta, citizens of both colors are beginning to celebrate our role in the history of the Civil Rights Movement. Here, Ray Charles famously walked out of a performance at the historic Bell Auditorium when he learned the crowd would be segregated. James Brown, who grew up on the streets of Augusta, would later proclaim to an international audience "I'm black and I'm proud!"

Another child of Augusta, a little black young lady by the name of Butterfly McQueen, used to sneak into the back door of the Modjeska Theatre here and watch the shows and movies. Butterfly would go on to become the classically trained actress, singer and dancer who won fame with her role in Gone With The Wind. After that movie, she made the ultimate stand for civil rights by turning and walking away from a Hollywood that insisted on typecasting her as the Negro maid. The legacy of bravery and brilliance of those people who made a stand against the evils of segregation would bring a tear of joy to the face of President Washington.

The fact is that what occurred in Washington's lifetime and in the lifetime of Woodrow Wilson still resonates today despite the will of the people to end the notion of second or third class citizenship. Culture evolves slowly so it is easy to pinpoint trends and identify why people or segments of society behave in certain manners.

For example, have you ever wondered why black families tend to choose unique or unusual names for their children? Watch the movie Roots and you will get your answer. Throughout the movie, the character of Kunta Kinte refuses to give up his name in exchange for the more European sounding "Toby." Kunta Kinte endures beatings over his refusal to submit to the name change.

In African society that period, and in many of the countries today, a child was not named until it had survived a full week. The father was charged with deciding the name of his offspring and it was one of the most important tasks of his life. To the Africans such as Kunta Kinte, the name of an individual was the most sacred thing they possessed. They believed and still do today that a person's name is part of the soul of the individual. The flamboyant singer, actor and drag queen RuPaul backs up the assertion of how an ancient cultural tradition survives over the centuries. Writing in his official bio, RuPaul, remembers his mother telling him she gave his the unusual name because she wanted him to be the only person in the world with that name. She wanted him to go on to superstardom and live up to his unique name. Entertainment history tells us that RuPaul did live up to his mothers wishes in an unconventional sort of way.

When searching for similarities in cultures, it is easy to make comparisons and many times the common link becomes apparent. While you don't find many white guys named RuPaul, Dale Carnegie wrote in his book How To Win Friends And Influence People:

"Remember that a person's name is to that person the sweetest and most important sound in any language."

Carnegie was a white guy, and he saw the importance of a name to a human being as something universal. So, that is something that black and white people share even though whites tend to name their children Scott and black people prefer something like Zequan. It is a commonality as humans that we share. The more we look at what we perceive as differences, we tend to find they are not differences at all.

In studying the evolution of culture, not only is it possible to discover similarities between segments of society, but it is also possible to pinpoint the roots and causes of current problems in the various segments. Comedian Bill Cosby is one of the very few black luminaries that have attempted to address the fact that in many segments of black society today the notion of being a father is virtually nonexistent.

Mr. Cosby understands that children, especially young males need a strong father in their lives. When young men have no father present in their lives, then it is natural they will search elsewhere for role models. The fact, and what Cosby opined, is that most inner city juvenile males without a father anywhere to be found end up turning to rappers who make millions of dollars promoting a lifestyle of crime in their music as role models. Eventually they emulate the behavior they hear in that music and join gangs. The gangs become the child's family and the end result is that child matures to a life of crime and ends up in the penal system or dead.

After he made statements decrying the loss of the black father, Bill Cosby caught hell from people of his own race. But the facts are simply there, no one can lay the blame at racist judges and juries for the reason that there are a hideously high percentage of black males in prison when statistically compared with the overall population percentages of America's racial makeup. There may be more white males total in the penal system, but when compared to population percentages, black males statistically fill more jail space.

In my career covering crime in Augusta, I have compiled my own data. For the crime of armed robbery, 9 in 10 armed robbers in the city of Augusta are black males between the ages of 18 and 30. How do I know this? When I call the police dispatch supervisor, I ask for certain information. I need to know the location, the time of the crime, whether or not an injury occurred in the commission of the crime and the Be On the Look Out data, or BOLO. After a specific period of time, the data I recorded was compiled to determine an empirical set of numbers and the numbers do not lie.

Now, that is not to say that plenty of white men commit all different types of crime, but an overwhelming majority of the specific crime of armed robbery in the city of Augusta are committed by young black males. The next step is to ask why this is so. Are black men predisposed genetically to rob people or is there a socioeconomic and cultural factor that is in play? Cosby argues that any unattended young male of any color that is allowed to run the streets and listen to violent music will create the atmosphere for that child to become a criminal. He says it is a lack of parenting, specifically the lack of a strong male presence in the adolescent's life. I agree and no one is genetically predisposed to commit crime.

The next question then is why are there a disproportionate number of black single parent families in which there is no father in the child's life? Notice I am not looking at divorced couples who co-parent, but a situation to where there is no father in the picture what-so-ever. The answer can easily be found in the cultural evolution within the black American experience over the span of history.

As stated earlier that in Africa it was a father's duty to name his child, when the people of Africa were kidnapped and brought to America, that sacred duty was taken away. In fact, all of the duties of the male parent were taken away. Black slave men did not name their children, the slave owner did.

Under slavery, marriage between two people of bondage was not recognized under the law. Now this is a hurtful fact to bring up, but it is a fact none the less. Slaves were counted as property. Under the law, a slave could be traded for legal tender. Under those rules, slaves were not allowed to marry any more than would two heads of cattle. The role of the father was diminished to that of sire, or baby-daddy. Black men of good "stock" were expected to have multiple partners because more children meant more profit to the owner. The sire of a child had absolutely no say in the matter if that child eventually was put up for sale. There evolved an emotional distance between child and father.

By the time of Segregation, the role of the black father had already been severely damaged and the socioeconomic factors of those early 20th Century days diminished it further. Many black men simply could not support a large family like their white counterparts could. Now, were there exceptions to this trend? Of course there were, and today we call those exceptions the black middle class.

James Brown never knew who his father was, and he struggled with it all his life. Butterfly McQueen's father, an educated stevedore, abandoned his family when she was just five years old. Unlike Brown, McQueen never committed a crime in her life; she went in the opposite direction because she had a mother that demanded she become educated. However, McQueen never trusted men intimately and never married or had children.

Our next door neighbor is my daughter's best friend and that poor child is caught in that cycle as well. I drive the kids to school each day and he comes over to play with Emmie every afternoon. He virtually spent the entire last summer over at my house. My daughter adores him.

It breaks my heart that his mother has 3 children all with different fathers. I hear the partying that emanates from the house next door and I know what is going on. I have tried to be a good role model to the child, but I am also a realist. While Emerson, who is 6 years old, says she will one day marry the little boy next door, I know that is not likely to happen. Nothing short than a miracle will keep that kid out of the cycle he is growing up in.

It is very sad.

The theory is that there is a disproportionate number of black males that are absentee fathers because it was something that was slowly conditioned in them over the span of several hundred years. It totally makes sense that a young male that grows up with no father is far more likely to become an absentee father himself.

Once the problem is identified and a root cause discovered, it becomes much easier to begin working towards a solution. Middle class whites and blacks look at the "gansta" culture as something degenerate that exists in a vacuum and to a degree it does. However, to solve the problem everyone must recognize the hard fact that the ghetto culture was created by centuries of a segment of society being oppressed. When black scholars maintain that white people set out to destroy black people, they are not all wet in their assertions. The white people of today must wrap their heads around the fact that the generations before did commit atrocities that have a direct impact on the mindsets of today.

Now, to bring this full circle, why does racism have a place in a book about fiscal conservatism? Why are we discussing gangsta culture along with a proposal to sever ties with the UN? The answer is that the real and perceived racial and social disparity is destroying our nation every bit as much as the UN is attempting to circumvent our sovereignty. In terms of the treasury, a disproportionate number of black males are in prison and it costs money to house them. Those absentee fathers leave behind children that must be fed and clothed by the taxpayers.

Americans of African heritage have already brought much to the American table. Given the chance, they can bring even more and enjoy their God given pursuit of happiness. That will never happen if white people do not acknowledge the struggles of the black race and if won't happen until the black leaders in America drop the race card in the trash bin help identify solutions.

In South Africa, the learned minds there created a Truth and Reconciliation Commission in the wake of Apartheid. The results of that Commission, some say, were mixed. However, it cannot be denied that people sat in front of a microphone and confessed their deeds. I do not believe reparations for slavery are necessary, but I think we, as a society, could use a good airing of the truth when it comes to segregation of the past.

At the end of the discussion, if it means that signs on the highways honoring Strom Thurmond and Robert Byrd must come down, then so be it. Take down the signs and allow history to record and reflect what they and many others like them really stood for. The same goes for people like Reverend Al Sharpton and former Georgia Congressional Representative Cynthia McKinney. Their lies and corrupt intentions must be exposed and tolerated no further. Black people of good conscience should rebuke them for holding their own race down while pandering to the economically disadvantaged for political and financial gain. The next time Sharpton shows up at the funeral of a thug that was killed in the commission of a crime and raises that individual up to be some kind of saint, he should be publicly shunned. The next time a black minister shouts "God Damn America" from his pulpit, the congregation should walk the hell out of the building.

Bill Cosby is a celebrated role model and Jesse Jackson is a seething, angry, obstructionist racist. Similarly, actor Mel Gibson is a racist pig who hates Jews and deserves to forever have empty seats in the theatres where his movies are shown. Those are simply the facts.

The ninth and final plank of the Contract On The Government is that a commission be established to once and for all investigate and put to rest what happened in America during the period of segregation.

The old saying is the truth will set you free, and it is finally time to drag this shameful part of our past out into the light of reason. We owe it to the heroes of the Civil Rights era, people like George Washington Carver, Ray Charles, James Brown, Butterfly McQueen and Martin Luther King Jr., to recognize their struggles beyond just erecting a memorial marker or designating month of learning. Those people are great Americans.

There are others, both white and black, who sacrificed everything they had so that our current generation can finally live up to ideals of the sacred documents we possess as a nation. Those documents espouse liberty for all who are citizens of the United States and before we can fully ratify those ideals in their totality, we must confront the wrongs of the past perpetrated against the citizens of this nation.

Lyrics from the band Pink Floyd reflect on the one little thing that finally separated humans from the rest of the animal kingdom and according to the progressive rockers that thing was: we learned to talk. An unbridled and transparent conversation on segregation is long overdue. In talking together, we will ultimately find a common ground. We share it. We did not create racism, we inherited it, and we do not have to pass it along to the next generation. The issue of race problems in America can be solved if we, black and white, are resolved to simply discuss our past candidly and move forward towards the future together.

A final thought, if you believe in heaven, then you will understand that it is not now and never was a segregated place. There is no such thing as a cordoned off paradise. Let's make our motto "as above, so below."

Chapter 10.
Why?

It is such an interesting little word of three characters that can be used as a word, a phrase or a sentence all by its lonesome. Asking "why" has over and again led to unlocking the secrets of the universe. So we will end this little journey together with that one word. Why should anyone care about what has been written here? Why does it matter that we must take our government back to its founding principles? Why shouldn't we just let the politicians do whatever it is that they do and go about our lives without caring?

The reason is simple. One day, you are going to die.

That fact may be jarring to you, but it is the truth. If you are reading this and breathing in air, then every breath you take simply gets you one breath closer to the last. As soon as anyone mentions the phrase "Judeo-Christian Ethics," there are some that recoil in terror. But in every book from every religion out there, the issue of the afterlife is addressed. Christians are not the only ones who believe death leads to the soul to finding either paradise or finding the exact opposite to live in for eternity. The atheists don't believe in an afterlife, but I have never heard one question whether or not death is real. Like gravity, death happens to everyone.

One aspect that we as a society in America have veered away from is the understanding and acceptance of our own death. If plastic surgery can keep us from looking like Grandma at age 90, then surely there must be a cure for death! Nowadays, the government has gotten into the act of trying to protect us against death. There are some out there that almost expect the government to prevent death from ever happening to them. The government can regulate the amount of sodium that a food vendor is allowed to sell to you, but that regulation only means you will eventually die with less sodium in your bloodstream. The regulation will not prevent your death.

From personal experience, I will maintain with you that death is unavoidable, but it is also not something to fear. Death is the reason you view a beautiful sunrise with awe. Death is the reason you mark how tall your kid is getting with little notches on the closet door jam. We live and make our mark in this world with the knowledge that our time is finite. Ben Franklin knew his time was limited and he used every waking moment to make the world around him a better place. Old Ben did not care that he would not be around to enjoy the fruits of his labor. He didn't care about his mortality, but rather strove to change the world while he was alive and that is precisely why we honor him.

So, now that we are discussing the awful scenario of the possibility that no one out there aside from God is immortal, then you must come to the understanding that the world will continue to go on after your death. When people warn of our children eventually paying for the present excesses of our nation, they are being serious in that they understand the bill will come due at some point in time. If you knew that you were to die a week from next Monday, would you go buy a Mercedes and throw a champagne and cocaine party with celebrities and then hand the credit card bill to your child as you choked out your last breath?

Of course you wouldn't.

Yet, as a society, that is exactly what we are doing. On the one hand, we feel the government should provide every possible avenue to us so that we might avoid dying. However, when it comes to paying the bill for said treatment, we automatically think that it will never come due in our lifetimes. What kind of a paradox is that?

The answer to why you should care is found in the faces of your children and your grandchildren. You are one day going to die and while you are still alive you do not really own any portion of the Earth, you are merely a steward of it until it is time for your progeny to step up to the plate. Then, they become stewards until the day that God determines they should breathe their last breath. And on, and on.

We cannot afford to leave our children with a bankrupt and broken system of government. We can't just sit back and think the current elected class is going to do anything other than continue on business as usual. A simple walk through history will show that no cycle of any kind in finite. Indeed, one of these days even the Earth herself will die when our Sun goes supernova.

Critics will likely point out that there is not one original thought being presented in this book and on that account they will be correct. Henry Ford did not invent the automobile either; he simply came up with a better method of assembly. While this book may lack original thought, it combines the thoughts of others into a framework that has not yet before been offered as a package to a public who are right now demanding governmental reform of some kind. And we must demand that reform happen in our lifetime; we owe it to our children to make it happen before we die.

The problems affecting America at the dawn of the 21st century are vast yet not unsolvable. There are different groups currently actively pursuing tax reform, welfare reform and fiscal conservatism in government spending. What has been missing in all the Tea Parties and Fair Tax rallies is a defining document or roadmap to rally behind. The brilliance of the Tea Party movement is that they kept the message simple allowing for Constitutionalists like me to enter the tent and espouse my ideas along with the famous politicians involved in hoisting the tent. My voice and yours can be heard in these venues and that is something that strikes fear in the heart of George Soros and those who hold the belief that they alone should own and control the world.

People are outraged at the excesses of Washington D.C. but have at this point no real list of priorities to demand of public officials. There so far has been no real cause to unify the various groups searching for a solution to the ills of this republic, and the momentum has taken decades to fully get underway. I do not call myself a Tea-Partier, but I feel I have much in common with the people in the movement. As I like to think of it, the person who believes in the Contract On The Government is one who understands the Judeo-Christian principle that humans work the will of God on Earth and not their own. That same principle states that the reward for that work will not come to us on Earth, but later, when we individually meet face to face with our God.

One might think that as the author of this book I should have spent more time researching and coming up with a brilliant new method of taxation that would be fair to middle class. Yet, while taxation is burdensome to us in the middle class, no new method of taxation is going to fix a government that cannot and will not spend the money it receives responsibly. After reviewing this book, people may come to the conclusion I should have spent time reviewing the socialized health care plan currently under works in Washington DC, or study the burden of illegal immigration that is causing some in the southwest to consider secession as an alternative to an unresponsive federal government.

Others still might think it would have been prudent to explain more about what Socialism is and why believers of this form of government are slowly destroying the nation that was founded on the concept of individualism. I suppose since the idea of gay marriage is such a big topic in the collective mind, there will be some that think I should have focused energy on that issue.

In one way or another, all of those things have been addressed in this book. If the Contract On The Government is followed, all of the second tier issues can be debated and settled using the same rationale I use every day deciding how to present a news story and that rationale is 'what would the reasonable person infer according to the law?' Logically, that line of thinking leads to the question of: how would the reasonable person react according to the law? Using a legal document to solve day-to-day problems is exactly how this republic was designed to function. The document that contains all of the answers is the one we call the United States Constitution.

Conservative pundits have over and over again complained that there is no singular charismatic voice out there to combine the various interested groups into one true populist uprising. If conservatives could dig Ronald Reagan up out of the ground and prop him up on a dais, they would do it in a heartbeat. In this book, you have not found that charismatic fellow who will go on television and echo the words of Reagan and attempt to guide the country back to bliss. I am not a politician and I never want to become one. For me, I follow the immortal words of one General Sherman, "if nominated I shall not run, if elected I shall not serve." Battling and exposing corruption in the local area in which I live is enough to fulfill my sense of purpose and I am not looking for a future in national politics.

The country does not need me, nor does it need to revive Reagan. What the country needs is for the individuals who call themselves the People to follow the examples set forth by George Washington. President Washington was a man of few words, but when he spoke, he did so with authority. When he warned of permanent alliances, the country needed to at the time and still does need to heed that warning. Washington set the benchmark on fiscal conservatism by paying down the Revolutionary era debt to France and refusing to allow that debt to be a cause for this nation to be permanently tied to France should she go to war with another nation.

Washington also understood a permanent military meant the eventual creation of an establishment that sold weaponry and could be a capitalistic mechanism that kept the United States in continued conflict just so that an arms industry could thrive. Washington warned in his writings of the very excesses we as a nation are allowing today.

It wasn't just George Washington who created the US Constitution; the document was the brainchild of a group of people who were among the greatest political thinkers of their time. However, it was George Washington who was the first man to implement the Constitution and the first to assume office under the power it possesses.

Washington read the words of Cicero and understood that even the new nation he helped create would face far more challenges other than what the British military offered. What he helped champion was the rule of law based upon the language contained in this republic's defining document. Washington exercised the power enumerated to him as President according to the Constitution and agreed what was not enumerated was a power not available to the national government. Washington stuck to his guns on that and all other matters that involved with the founding principles of his republic. Washington knew that democracy was impossible, but democratic principles were sacred.

We do not need a new Reagan to unify the people who understand that this republic is in trouble and are seeking answers to the problems we, as a nation, are facing. We need to unify ourselves and demand our elected leaders follow the document that sets our principles into law. They must follow the document that was ratified as being law. The road map to get back to that point as sovereign people in control of our own government is this Contract On The Government.

For those who like to read the ending of a book before actually reading the book, the Contract is as follows:

1   Repeal the 17th Amendment.

2   Give the President a Constitutional line item veto on

budgetary matters.

3   **Codify the War Powers Act as an Amendment and turn national intelligence gathering responsibilities to the military in accordance to the Constitution.**

4   **Curtail domestic welfare by amending the Constitution granting voting rights to taxpayers only.**

5   **Curtail foreign welfare to be given only to emerging trading partners of the United States.**

6   **Withdraw totally from the United Nations and declare the U.S. a sovereign power with no permanent alliances.**

7   **Reduce the federal bureaucracy by eliminating all agencies that operate in violation of the 10th Amendment of the US Constitution.**

8   **Establish an Amendment to the Constitution that declares the budget of the United States will, each year, will be balanced. Congress will also commit to a 10% reduction in all non-essential spending over the next five year period, including their salaries.**

9   **Establish a commission to examine and expose the details of legal segregation that occurred in the United States during the 19th and 20th centuries and give all parties immunity from prosecution.**

If you believe those planks listed here need to be enacted and followed by the elected men and women of this country, then you are not a Democrat or a Republican, you are not a Tea Partier or a Fair Taxer and you are not a liberal or a conservative. What you are is a believer of Washingtonian Constitutionalism. As such, you now have a blueprint and a roadmap in the form of this Contract from which you now must make your stand.

I believe that everyone has a purpose. No matter what it is you do in life, your actions do at some point impact others and, therefore, you as an individual do have a purpose. It is my belief and understanding that sometimes an individual's purpose might be to present an example to others to not to make the same choices the particular individual made that resulted in tragedy. In my community, a fellow by the name of Justin Elmore was such an individual. Justin could not abide by the law and eventually those charged with enforcing the law had to intervene and shoot him dead during the commission of a crime.

136

Luminaries such as Reverend Al Sharpton attended Justin Elmore's funeral and there was a near riot that occurred locally over this man's death. But then after the dust settled, people sat back and thought about it and realized that Justin had himself put into motion the events that ended in his violent death. I do not know why God chose Justin to make such a point to society, as a reporter I was just one of many who were there covering the event. In fact, it may have been Justin and not God that chose his purpose. No matter what, that purpose was fulfilled. We all have free will and Justin used his free will to his own peril.

After the rhetoric was over at the funeral, reason converged on the people still alive in Justin's wake. In his tragic life and death, Justin did indeed fulfill his purpose of presenting a warning to all.

"Please don't make the same mistakes I made," Justin said to all from the grave. It is difficult to grasp that even a criminal has a greater purpose, but it must be considered and thought out when each of us consider our own lives and why we, as individuals, matter. As individuals we can be highlighted as part of the problem or part of the solution and it is our own individual decisions that shape where we stand. We must all realize that at some point everyone who lives and draws breath eventually is forced or coerced into making a stand of some kind before we die.

While you may only have one vote, you do as a member of this society and a child of, let's just say, a sovereign creator, have a purpose. You can be a bystander or you can be an instigator or you can be a criminal or the next charismatic public figure that comes along and wows the masses; but you, as one, do have a purpose that you will eventually go on to fulfill. It is my solemn desire that I may now come to the conclusion that my purpose on Earth has been fulfilled as I have now finished writing The Contract On The Government. Yet, I come to the conclusion that my purpose on Earth has been fulfilled as I have now finished writing The Contract On The Government. Yet, I know God doesn't exactly work that way. While I would like to retire my keyboard and get back to the fun I have raising chickens and camping outdoors, I know there will be more work for me concerning these matters when the sun rises again.

I am ready.

Let us get to work at doing what we can, according to our own individual purpose, and we will all sleep well each night knowing we tried our best. Help me join with others to take the Contract to Washington, D.C. and force its implementation.

Revolutions can be peaceful as Dr. King proved. In our time, we have it in our grasp to change what is occurring in our nation without resorting to armed conflict to settle the issues.

One hundred years from now the people living will judge us on our actions and I hope they conclude we did what was right and proper and that we acted in a manner that was consistent with our core beliefs that the Constitution of the United States is the greatest legal document ever written.

"Iceberg, right ahead!"

…Oh, and have a nice day…

Acknowledgments

It takes a village to compile this much information into a readable tome, especially when the writer just happens to be the village idiot. Therefore, some acknowledgements are in order.

A bottomless crevasse worth of respect goes to Christopher Hudson, Van Hudson, Woody and Ange Merry and Lee and Patty Miller for spending hours on the telephone with me debating the issues and then slogging through the early manuscripts catching every conceivable problem with the content. Former Columbia County Judge Bobby Christine spent hours editing the manuscript and offering suggestions.

BJ Wood, editorial cartoonist of the Columbia County News/Times newspaper did an amazing job of drawing the cover art and adding in the tongue-in-cheek elements. BJ also rocks the sure shot on the drums.

Austin Rhodes, a talk show host for WGAC radio, added tremendously to this book simply by espousing his own ideas on the air and following up with me off the air with research and advice.

There were some people with PhD's that aided in this writing. While they may or may not agree with my political views, Dr. Hubert van Tuyll and Dr. Debra van Tuyll were tremendous assets to me in learning the history of the United States, military history, and the ethics that makes for a good reporter.

Along with the van Tuyll's at Augusta State University is Peter Flanagan who I give credit for my understanding and interpretation of Constitutional law. Dr. Michael (Cowboy Mike) Searles of ASU got me interested in black history and led me to explore more fully the role black Americans have played in making the United States what it is today. I am forever in his debt for exposing me to the heroes that lived once on the grounds I walk every day. These people signed off on my degree - which either proves my authority on the matters discussed in this book, or proves that I too have been educated way beyond my intelligence.

Mary Liz Nolan, News Director at WGAC radio/Beasley Broadcasting has been my rock, my lighthouse and my harbor for years. My Friend Benjie Westafer has been instrumental in getting the book formatted and the appropriate website created to get the word out to the public. So, thanks Benj.

Thank you to all of you who have worn the banner of the United States on your sleeve. Thank you for your service to this country and your commitment to the liberty envisioned by the Framers of our Constitution. We, as Americans, should all forever be grateful for the sacrifices given by our armed forces that began even before Valley Forge and continues to this day.

Thank you too Crispus Attucks, I haven't forgotten you.

About the Author

Tommy Scott Hudson is an award winning investigative reporter for heritage radio station WGAC AM/FM in Augusta, Georgia and writes continuously for The Verge and Buzz On Biz publications. Mr. Hudson has worked as a special correspondent for CBS Radio News and The BBC. Mr. Hudson along with Debra Reddin VanTuyll were co-editors of the book "Augusta's WGAC: The Voice of the Garden City for 70 Years" which won the Best Depiction of Georgia History Award from the Georgia Department Of Archives.